Negar Rezaee Aghbash

General Principles of Architectural Engineering,

Negar Rezaee Aghbash

General Principles of Architectural Engineering,

Design, Construction and Materials

Noor Publishing

Imprint

Any brand names and product names mentioned in this book are subject to trademark, brand or patent protection and are trademarks or registered trademarks of their respective holders. The use of brand names, product names, common names, trade names, product descriptions etc. even without a particular marking in this work is in no way to be construed to mean that such names may be regarded as unrestricted in respect of trademark and brand protection legislation and could thus be used by anyone.

Cover image: www.ingimage.com

Publisher:
Noor Publishing
is a trademark of
Dodo Books Indian Ocean Ltd. and OmniScriptum S.R.L publishing group

120 High Road, East Finchley, London, N2 9ED, United Kingdom
Str. Armeneasca 28/1, office 1, Chisinau MD-2012, Republic of Moldova, Europe
Printed at: see last page
ISBN: 978-620-5-63437-0

General Principles of Architectural Engineering, Design, Construction and Materials

By

Negar Rezaee Aghbash

Master of Architecture, Khatam University, Tehran, Iran

Negar Rezaee Aghbash

Master of Architecture, Khatam University, Tehran, Iran

Dedicated to the merciful angels who:

The lord of the worlds, who began to guide his servants with the teaching of the pen.

My parents, whose presence is a crown of honor for me and their name is a reason for my existence because these two existences after the lord, have been the source of my existence, took my hand and taught me to walk in this valley full of ups and downs.

Content

Chapter I

Introduction

Introduction

Today, housing is apparently only a place to live, not for the mental and emotional peace of family members. Because many of the profit seekers and material worshipers of the western world design a house that is the only source of their profit, and soul and spirit have become meaningless for them, and only its luxurious and seductive appearance is the priority, and this is exactly the opposite of Iranian architecture.

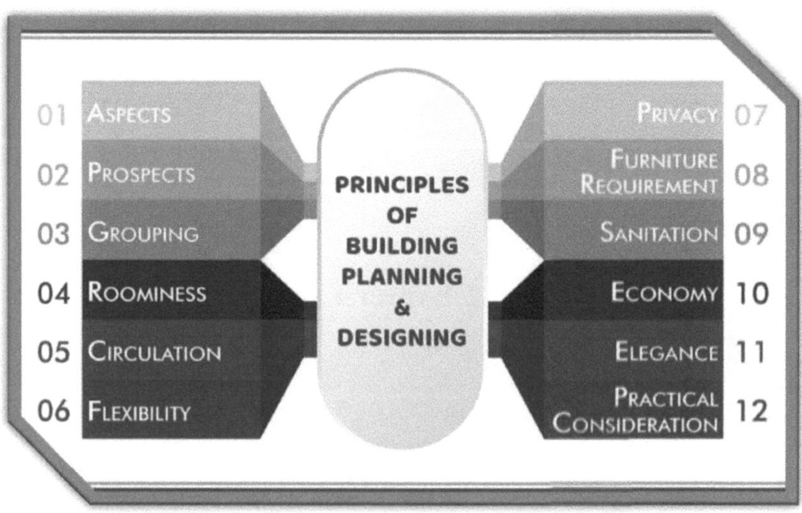

Figure 1. Principles of Building Planning/Designing

It is Islamic that yesterday an Iranian architect, builder, built a house with the people and for the people, the soul and life and peace of the family was his first goal, and the residence was placed in the second degree of importance, and unfortunately worldliness, appearance, and utilitarianism. Today, the western world is infiltrating our architectural culture and institution, and some architects educated in western schools or more importantly, build and sell profiteers who only think about their own profit and property, welcome it, and those architectural measures are alien to this. Merz and Bom are implemented as the most modern facilities today for the well-being of users. Today's architecture has intentionally or unintentionally fallen on a path that takes us away from its origin, and it seems that some people in the society blindly think that it is a satisfactory answer to their desires.

It is necessary to emphasize that at the beginning we must make it clear that we are not against the development of architecture and the use of the latest facilities in building construction. We are only trying to prevent its conflict with our culture and instead of pure imitation of western culture and appearance, we are trying to make it compatible with our national-shari'a and cultural standards, and we are trying to reduce its disadvantages and strengthen its potential advantages and in in this direction, let's rediscover our architectural identity.

The main goal is that our architecture does not become more westernized. Because if our architecture becomes westernized, the foothold of western industrial products for consumption in the country will become so strong that our market will eventually become westernized and as a result we will lose our national identity and trust in all supplies and become completely dependent on the west. If the house is built in a western style, its materials will also be western, and the decoration of the house will be western instead of plastering and tiling.

The western covering and decor of the house, in turn, will make the owner of the house look western, either intentionally or unintentionally, and it won't be long before we have to look for authentic culture and architecture and ancient values in museums and historical books. When the natural rotation of the wind through wind deflectors, which itself is an evolved example of green and sustainable architecture, gives way to fan coil circulation, even meeting our cooling and heating needs depends on the help of the west, and the west only when it gives us It helps us to be westerners and subject to the demands of Westerners, and this means completely losing our Iranian Islamic identity. It should be noted that we are not against technology either, but we should reduce its negative and costly effects and not depend on it, and instead make the most of free natural energies that are also economical.

Professor Mohammad Karim Pirnia has emphasized the existence of five principles in Iranian house-building and architecture, which are: introversion, people-orientedness, avoiding futility, self-sufficiency, and self-sufficiency. These five principles, which in simpler terms were: creating privacy, having a human scale, beneficial use and avoiding creating something just for beauty, the use of organic materials, stability and construction techniques today with the increasing prevalence of foreign architecture and culture that It is completely uncoordinated and not paying attention to the climate and texture of the region, they are gradually forgotten.

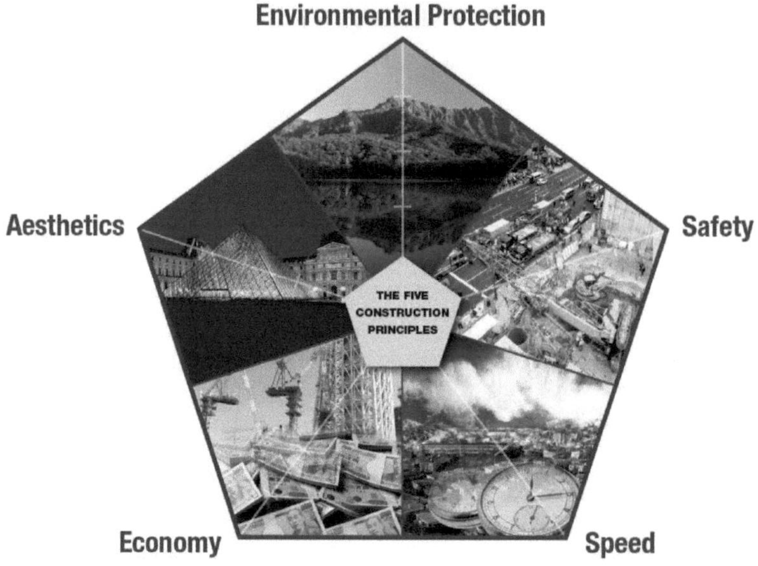

Figure 2. The Five Construction Principles

Urban spaces with those identity less buildings and mostly stone facades in the style of classical European architecture are expanding day by day in the urban context, and it seems that architecture in Iran has no significant background and past, and Iranians in the field architecture has done nothing but pure imitation.

At the same time, our traditional solutions, such as wind deflectors in Kashan houses, are used as ventilation agents in high-rise buildings around the world. Instead of taking advantage of this huge and rich achievement of our architecture, we have turned to blindly imitating it and not in harmony with the culture and the environment, and every day we are destroying our architectural identity more and more. Although we are forced to build apartments due to the increase in population and lack of land, we are not forced to build in the European way.

Still, one or two-story houses and so-called villas are built in the corners of this border, especially in the noble neighborhoods, and unfortunately, most of them are built in an alien way. This research tries to identify and investigate and finally design a two-story house in an authentic and magnificent Iranian-Islamic style and manner, according to today's needs with past climatic solutions. It is hoped that, in this regard, we will once again witness the rediscovery of our lost identity in architecture and its place as a special and independent method in the world.

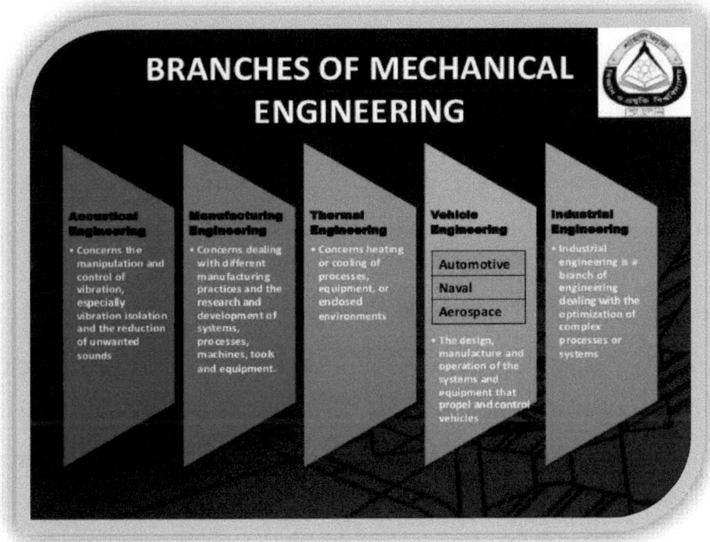

Figure 3. Engineering, Design, Architecture

Home

The house is actually a form of privacy and privacy is the creation of boundaries. Privacy is not separation, but creates veils and prevents the encroachment of others. Privacy is the smoothness of the communication network. Privacy is not only confirmed in social relationships, but it can be found in the way men and women coexist, in the arrangement of the home, in the arrangement of the urban space, in the garden, in dressing, and even in the chastity of speech. Among the spaces that exist as privacy around us, the house is the most immediate space related to a person that affects him and affects him on a daily basis. It is the first space in which a person experiences the sense of spatial belonging. The set of five senses constantly goes through its head and gets used to it in a short period of time. In fact, the house is a place where more than half of a person's life is spent, and this shows its importance in a person's life.

Iranian

In the architecture of the house in ancient Iran, the attention of the architects to the special structure of the spaces of the house and the communication between their components with mystical insight and semiotics is behind the artistic architecture. The coordination of relations between the structure of house components in Iran in terms of form, color and geometric elements with Iranian mystical principles and the specific worldview of architecture. For example, the use of the dome is related to the understanding of the universe and its beyond, according to the vision of the architect.

Islamic

What separates the architecture of Muslim houses from other residential houses in the world is the respect for people and space in the definition of a special concept of home to express the concept of residence. In other words, the Qur'an and the Sunnah contain a coherent list of sources that can provide us with a set of basic principles as a guide and framework for the design of housing architecture. In other words, the design of a Muslim's house should be the result of the Islamic values and beliefs of its residents.

Iranian-Islamic house

While the traditional arts are diverse and multiplicity in form and meaning, they imply common concepts. As one of the main traditional arts of Iran, traditional architecture contains rich concepts that are formed based on the beliefs of the people of this land. The secret of creation, the hierarchy of existence and heaven are among the most important concepts that have caused the formation of such architecture. Meanwhile, the house is very important as the main architectural space and as a place where people spend most of their lives.

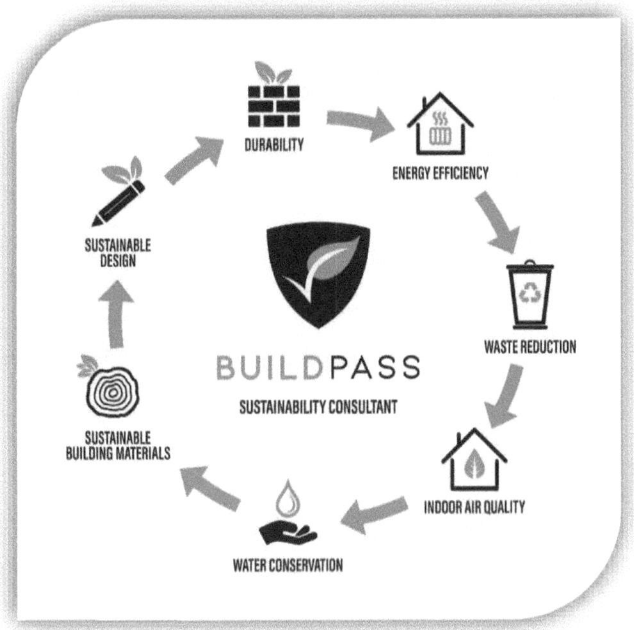

Figure 4. The 7 principles of sustainable construction

A person who sees life as a path to perfection has undoubtedly tried to create an environment that will help him to achieve this goal. For this reason, the house in Iran is the right place to search for the beliefs that shaped it. Today, the architecture of most Iranian houses is limited to only four corners, which are dormitories and not a beautiful place to live. The goal should be to build well, and building well has three conditions: product, strength, and service, and the important thing is that these three features have an internal relationship, and in this context, the spaces of traditional houses were more efficient than modern houses.

The main goal in designing this house is to revive beliefs and traditions in Iranian house building. Because today our architecture is not only in house building, but in all fields, it has turned to western ways and especially copying the classic European facades, and unfortunately these facades have created identity lessness in Iranian architecture, the goal is that beauty the knowledge of Iranian architecture and the symbolism of its facades are known to the general public.

Perhaps such a house is more compatible with the needs and climate of Iran and will help to regulate the environmental conditions. Among other things, reviving the use of wind turbines in the dry and semi-desert climate of Iran or using the central courtyard in a new and more efficient way can give Iranian-Islamic architecture a renewed identity. Considering that today we are facing the prevalence of apartment building in Iran, in such a situation, we may not be able to revive most of the traditions in them, unless we implement its facade using the lasting elements of the past and perpetuate our past identity.

However, houses that are built in the so-called villas, and we are more or less facing them in all parts of Iran, can be a good option in this regard. Especially, the appearance and architecture of such houses have always attracted the attention of the public and in many cases, they have been used as a model for the design of subsequent houses.

An attitude on the principles of house building in Iranian architecture

Iran's art and architecture have long had several principles that are well shown in the examples of this art. Professor Mohammad Karim Pirnia has emphasized the existence of five principles in Iran's house building and architecture, and these principles are as follows: people-centeredness, avoiding futility, modesty, self-sufficiency, and introversion. These five principles are observed in the best possible way in all the buildings built in the past of Iran and can be easily seen.

In the following, we will have an attitude on these five principles. Wari people means observing the fit between the building organs and the human organs and paying attention to his needs in the construction work. Various people are visible in the parts of the building and its parts, for example, the three-door room, which is mostly used for sleeping, is enough to meet the needs of a family. Components such as doors and windows, shelves and posts used for bed storage also had suitable sizes. In Iranian architecture, they try not to work in vain in building and avoid extravagance. This principle has been observed both before Islam and after it. If in other countries arts related to architecture, such as painting and stone carving, are considered decorative, this has never been the case in our country.

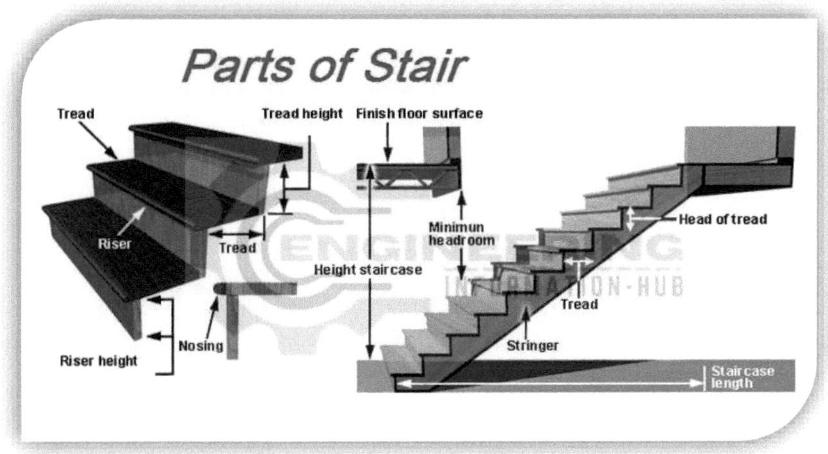

Figure 5. Stairs Types of stairs and Principles of Designing of Stairs

Making knots with plaster, tiles, clay and bricks, and according to Amod and Andod architects themselves, is part of the basic work of the building, and if a dome from Tizeh to Pakar is covered with tiles, it is not only for beauty. It should be known that the word "beautiful" means being beautiful and fitting, not beautiful. Niarash has been called static knowledge, construction technology and construction (material) science. Architects of the past paid a lot of attention to the appearance of the building and did not consider it separate from beauty.

They had gained experience and sizes for covers, openings, and holes, all based on the Niarash. Pimon was small and uniform sizes that were used wherever there was a need for it. Along with the use of pimon and repeating it in sizes and shapes, the architects used the buildings in many different ways.

No two buildings were the same, and each one had its own characteristics, although they followed the same pattern. Iranian architects tried hard, got the building they needed from the nearest places, and built such a building that they did not need the building of other places and were self-sufficient. In this way, the construction work is done more quickly and the building has become more compatible with the surrounding nature, and the building has always been available during its renovation. Basically, people's beliefs have been very effective in organizing various parts of buildings, especially traditional houses. One of the beliefs of Iranian people is valuing personal life and its sanctity, as well as the azan of Iranians, which has made Iranian architecture introverted.

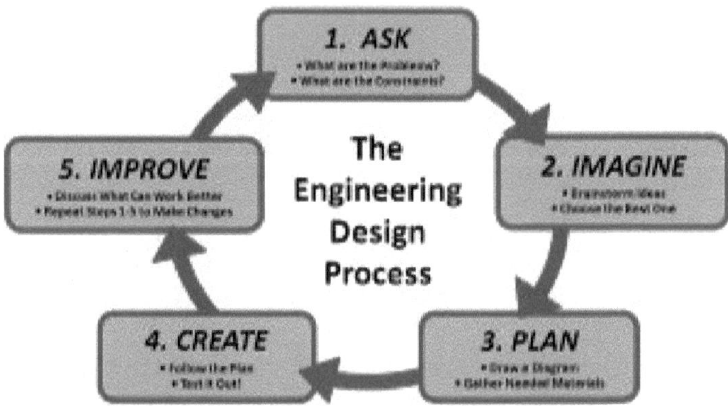

Figure 6. Engineering Design Process

An attitude on the principles of house orientation in the past

One of the important issues related to urban planning is the location of the house. This is related to the weather, the way of radiation for pleasant winds, storms, tornadoes, and the location and the type of land. Iranian architects have used a hexagonal shape for this. The old book Al-Masalek and Al-Mamalek Istakhari has maps in the appendix that are extremely beautiful. In these maps, the sign of south is placed on top of it and the opposite direction is north. Basically, this shape is obtained from this hexagon, which is placed at the vertices of the rectangle inside it, north and south. With the same method, three runes are considered in Iran:

- ✓ Ron rasteh.
- ✓ Ron Isfahani
- ✓ Ron Kermani

In Ron, the rectangle inside the hexagon has a northeast-southwest direction.

In the central cities of Iran such as Tehran, Yazd, Jahrom and Tabriz city in the northwest of Iran and some other cities, Raste rune has been used. The direction of this rune is almost facing the Qibla. At the beginning of Islam, in these places, there was no problem with the direction of the buildings towards the Qibla. Unfortunately, recently, by not considering this issue and with a new east-west orientation, they have built houses that should be left in the hot season due to the extreme heat. New Tehran has also fallen into its worst situation due to lack of attention to the right direction.

Knowing the elements of the Iranian house in the past

Panam is very important in architecture. In the houses, vertical and horizontal panams have been used in relation to the considered runes and the movement of the sun and the disturbances caused by its sting and heat. The use of sashes, radiating bands, vaulting and other things are examples of it. The three doors were also made so that the sun could not directly penetrate into them. Unfortunately, as it was said, in the Qajar period, various elements entered our architecture.

The three doors have been converted into two doors and they have made it so that the sun enters the room exactly. Lighting from the ceiling is another way to avoid direct sunlight to some spaces. The old architects believed that there was enough sunlight outside the house and did not feel the need to have it in the rooms of the house in the same way. In the oldest houses, whether large aristocratic houses or small rural and urban houses, part of the light was taken from the ceiling.

In addition, this type of lighting along with the soft color of the wall and ceiling of the rooms creates a good relaxation. On the other hand, due to blinding the western front of the house and preventing direct sunlight in the afternoons, the spaces behind this part received light from the roof, and the same is applied to other spaces such as the kitchen, the pool, due to the lack of access to direct light.

Arsen Khanah includes different spaces that have changed according to the type of house, in other words, the simplicity of the spaces, the use of large and small pimon and small pimon in the construction of houses by referring to the above sizes, it can be seen that this size was based on the human scale and the size of Iranian people. The height of the doors was as high as an average man.

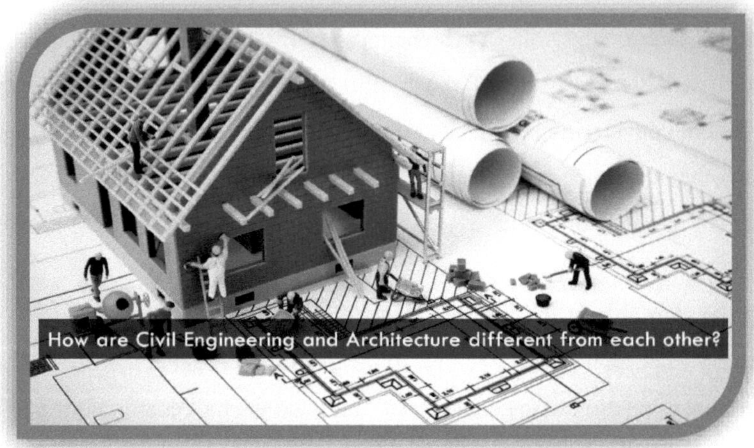

Figure 7. Civil vs Architecture Engineering, what is the Difference?

At the foot of the door, they used to put a threshold, which had various reasons, such as being careful to enter so that their heads did not hit up and showing respect by bending down, as well as preventing shoes and dirt from entering the corridor and other things that were there. Is. In the plan of the rooms, courtyards, etc., they were helped by the Iranian golden proportion. Iranian golden ratio is obtained from a rectangle inside a hexagon.

The shape of the yard has five doors, three doors and other elements based on this proportion. Most of the houses, especially the luxurious ones, had a front door. Usually, the outer walls are made of straw and only the luxurious entrance is built. The ratio of the width to the indentation of the headboard was usually one to two. The components of the headboard consisted of frames and frames on it. If the width is wide in the middle frame, it is squared.

Chapter II

Theoretical foundations of energy saving in architecture with an energy saving approach

Collecting is natural in a person, and taste and taste in collecting will undoubtedly always be with him. In our modern society, the museum represents the institutionalization of the general tendency to collect. The museum in its present form was founded by Ptolemy in Alexandria in the late 3rd century BC, but in the Middle Ages the educational role of museums faded due to the dominance of the Church and the Inquisition. With the beginning of the renaissance and the flourishing of sciences, museums began their activities in parallel with the growth and development of various sciences.

During the 19th and 20th centuries, the expansion of museums caused education to be recognized as one of the functions of the museum and the activity in various fields of art, culture and education in the museum became more and more fruitful. Now are the golden years of museum architecture in the world. The architectural works of museums in the world are done with more thought and force of thought.

New museums are designed to accommodate more visitors and create more traction, as well as attract more attention. The museum has always been a cultural and research center, but now, in addition to all this, it is a gathering, cultural-artistic learning, a center for selling objects made or printed by museums, as well as a boutique, amphitheater, restaurant, and more use of sound technology and is the image One of the deficiencies that can be seen in our architecture today is the lack of a specialized center for architecture. Such a center can be suitable for the gathering of architects and architecture enthusiasts and students.

This center can be a place to hold architectural conferences, specialized meetings, critique and review architectural works of the world, design and hold architectural competitions, learn about new design technologies, plan and organize an architecture film festival. This place can also strive to preserve and maintain valuable architectural works as well as the works of great architects. In addition, in this center, one can try to conduct research on the current needs of the country's architecture and find solutions for them.

Although Iran is considered one of the oil-rich countries in the world and has huge resources of natural gas, fortunately due to the intensity of the sun's radiation in most areas of the country, the implementation of mandatory solar projects and the possibility of using solar energy in cities and sixty thousand Scattered villages across the country can bring significant savings in oil and gas consumption.

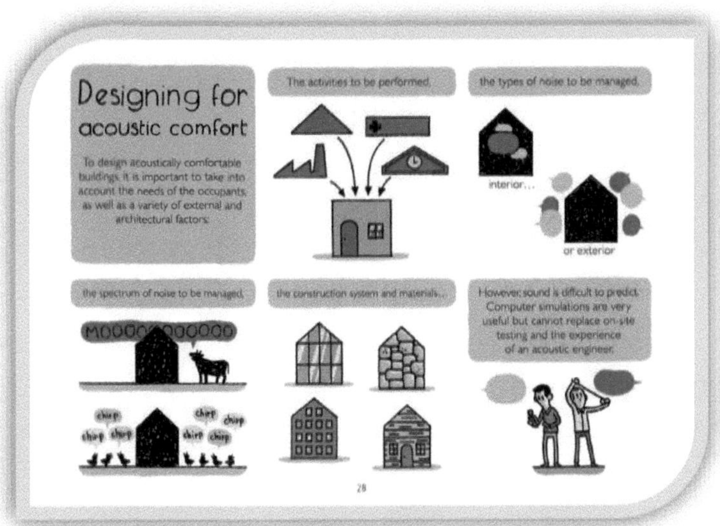

Figure 8. Basic Principles of Acoustics: Why Architects Shouldn't Leave It All to Consultants

Simple technology, not polluting the air and environment, and most importantly saving fossil fuels for future generations or turning them into valuable materials and artifacts using petrochemical techniques are the main reasons that reveal the necessity of using solar energy for our country. Converting solar energy in any form is desirable, but the economic possibilities of different plans must be carefully measured.

Today, it is technologically possible to use the sun's thermal energy to heat homes. Economically, due to the ever-increasing price of fossil fuels and other energy sources and the efforts of experts in reducing the cost of raw materials and equipment needed to collect heat and solar rays, researchers and scientists have been encouraged to study and optimize solar systems. Important progress has also been achieved.

Energy

Energy is the ability to do work by humans or other bodies, and work is called the source of power. From a scientific point of view, energy can be defined as follows: energy is the amount of ability that is consumed in a certain time of a task. This definition can be shown by the following relationship that when you pick things up or open a door or write something or ride a bicycle, you have used energy. Energy can be seen in different forms in nature, such as wind energy, vegetable fuel energy, earth energy, nuclear energy, hydrogen energy, radiation energy and sound energy and combined energies that can be the combination of any force with other forces.

History of renewable energy

According to the predictions of scientists and the international energy agency, the demand for energy consumption and production will increase rapidly and alarmingly in the future. So, that from 1998 to 2010, the global demand for electricity will reach 20,582 terawatts with a 30% increase and 27,326 terawatts with a 50% increase. On the other hand, according to scientists' studies, wind power will provide 20% of the world's electricity by 2040. Iran always has special national programs in terms of its geographical scope and environmental diversity in the energy sector.

Types of renewable energy

- ❖ *Solar energy:* on sunny days, the space inside the building is heated. The heat inside the buildings, caused by the penetration of the sun's radiant energy through the glass of the windows, acts like a greenhouse and prevents it from going outside and heats the room. Also, solar energy heats the walls and the top of the roof. This type of heating is called indirect solar heating.

❖ *Plant fuel energy:* green plants convert light energy into chemical energy during the process of photosynthesis. Plant burns can be converted into liquid, alcohol, and gases such as methane. These fuels are more efficient than wood. Because they are far less energy source and occupy less space. Animals get the food they need through plants. Vegetable fuel is indestructible.

❖ *Wind energy:* electricity can be made from wind energy. When the earth's air is cold, the air contracts and rushes down, but when the air is warm, the air expands and goes up. Therefore, warm air rises and cold air replaces it, and this is the moving air that is caused by the sun, which is called wind.

Figure 9. Engineering for sustainable development: delivering on the Sustainable Development Goals

❖ *Water energy:* Water is used to run machines. Water mills are built by the river. A part of the water flow of the river is directed through the pipe to the water turbines, which drives them, and electricity is produced due to the rotation of the water turbines, which are connected to the electricity generators. It is suitable to build a dam in places with steep slopes or high valleys. The benefits of water energy are: Hydro turbines do not use any fuel and produce no pollution.

❖ *Nuclear energy:* In 1896, nuclear energy was discovered by a scientist named Henri Becquerel. Currently, there are about 420 nuclear power plants, a quarter of which are located in the United States. In this power plant, they produce electricity from the heat of nuclear fuel. The only difference between a nuclear power plant is the type of fuel and how it is heated. Fuels such as fossil fuels must be burned to release their stored energy, but nuclear power plants produce energy without being burned.

❖ *Earth's thermal energy:* Earth's thermal energy is the heat that exists naturally under the earth and can be converted into electrical energy. The electricity obtained in this way is called the thermal energy of the earth.

❖ *Fossil energy:* less than 150 years ago, the first attempts to industrially extract oil began. The invention of the automobile and its popularity in the early 20th century expanded the dependence on oil. The outbreak of world war 1914 to 1918 made the importance of controlling oil resources clear. Petroleum products such as gasoline and diesel are used to run internal combustion engines.

❖ *Coal and gas energy:* Coal is used in factories and locomotives. The Chinese used coal to make copper about 3000 years ago. 7 centuries later, Greeks and Romans started using coal. Research shows that the early inhabitants of Britain used coal long before the Romans invaded this land in 55 BC.

❖ *Hydrogen energy:* 75% of the mass of materials and more than 90% of the atoms that make up nature are hydrogen. Hydrogen is a chemical element represented by the letter H and atomic number 1. Hydrogen is an element, colorless and odorless and non-metallic, monovalent and diatomic gas with high flammability. Hydrogen is the lightest and most abundant element in the world and is found in water and in the organic compounds of living organisms.

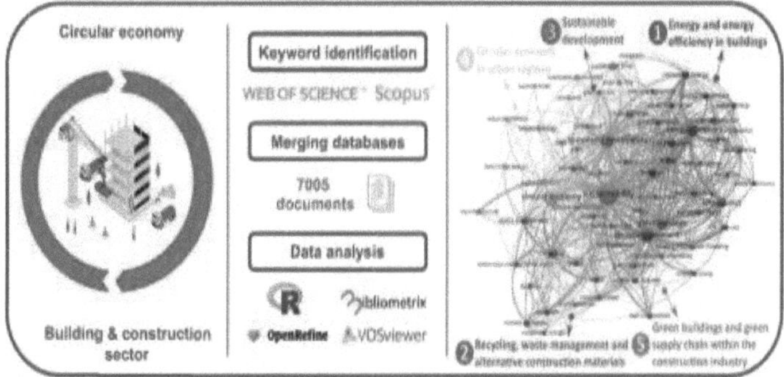

Figure 10. Circular economy in the building and construction sector: A scientific evolution analysis

Solar Energy

Solar energy is the most unique source of renewable energy in the world and is the main source of all energy on earth. The earth is located at a distance of 150 million kilometers from the sun and it takes 8 minutes and 18 seconds for the sunlight to reach the earth. Therefore, the contribution of the earth in receiving energy from the sun is a small amount of its total radiant energy.

The origin of all the different forms of energy known so far includes fossil fuels stored in the earth, wind energy, waterfalls, sea waves, etc., available on the planet from the sun. Solar energy, like other energies, can be directly or indirectly converted into other forms of energy. With about 300 sunny days per year, Iran is one of the best countries in the world in terms of solar energy potential. Considering the geographical position of Iran and the dispersion of villages in the country, the use of solar energy is one of the most important factors that should be considered. The use of solar energy is one of the best ways of electricity supply and energy production compared to other models of energy transmission to villages and remote areas in the country in terms of cost, transportation, maintenance and similar factors.

According to international standards, if the average solar radiation energy per day is higher than 305 kilowatt hours per square meter, the use of solar energy models such as solar collectors or photovoltaic systems is very economical and cost-effective. In many parts of Iran, the radiant energy of the sun is much higher than this international average, and in some places, it has been measured even higher than 7 to 8 kilowatt hours per square meter, but on average, the radiant energy of the sun on the surface of Iran is about 405 kilowatts. hours per square meter. The surface temperature of the sun is about 10,000 degrees Celsius, which is 3 times the melting point of steel, and the sun burns 770 million tons of hydrogen every second.

Figure 11. Neighborhood

Benefits of solar energy

- ✓ The consumption of fossil fuels is saved.
- ✓ Solar energy does not cause any pollution.
- ✓ Solar energy never runs out and saves fossil energy.

There are different ways to use solar energy, which can be divided into 4 general categories

- ❖ Inactive solar system.
- ❖ active solar system:
- ❖ Solar heating system.
- ❖ Photovoltaic system.
- ❖ Also, there are two ways of using solar energy in the building:
  - ❖ Active.
  - ❖ Passive:

Passive

In the passive solar system, the buildings are designed in such a way that the needs of cooling, heating and lighting are provided in a natural way and compatible with the climate, and for this reason, they are called passive systems that require the operation of the equipment. Cooling and heating are minimized. 2,400 years ago, Socrates found that today, with south-facing houses, the sun's rays penetrate the veranda in the winter, but in the summer, the sun's path is directly overhead, or above the roof, so that it creates shadows.

Therefore, the south side should be made bigger and longer to catch the winter sun, and the north side should be made shorter to avoid the winter winds. The heating strategy in the passive solar system is formed based on the amount of solar heat received, the amount of storage and how this heat is distributed and maintained. To optimize receiving solar heat in buildings that are equipped with a passive solar system, the following issues should be considered:

- ✓ Glass receiving surfaces should be placed on the south face.

✓ The direction of the openings is the most important factor to maximize solar heat gain.

✓ Orientation more than 25 degrees to the east or west reduces the effect of horizontal canopies and gradually reduces the amount of heat received.

✓ Passive solar systems, which are easy to build and implement, are usually integrated into the building envelope. Their materials are often common construction materials and the purpose of this system is to collect solar energy, store it properly and finally distribute energy in the interior spaces of the building to create comfortable conditions with the least possible heat loss.

Figure 12. The World's 20 Best Cities for Architecture Lovers

The main passive solar systems are:

❖ Direct receipt.

❖ Trump wall.

❖ Atrium.

❖ Glass chambers attached to the building.

❖ Heavy wall.

❖ Thermosiphon phenomenon.

❖ Glass balconies.

Direct receiving system

It is the simplest passive solar system. In this system, sunlight enters the interior from windows, openings, and skylights and is absorbed by interior surfaces and furniture. Buildings with direct absorption depend on south-facing windows called solar windows. Sunlight passes through the glass with short wavelength waves and enters the desired space. After these waves are radiated on the internal surfaces, they heat them and cause long wavelength waves to be emitted. These waves are no longer able to pass and are trapped inside the space, which is known as the greenhouse phenomenon. The heavy wall in this solar heat system is directly stored by a wall that has a high thermal capacity, such as a (concrete wall) and distributed in the interior spaces. When using the direct solar gain method, the floor of the building plays a very important role. Because in this case, the floor receives the sun's radiation as an intermediary.

Trompe wall

This system is similar to the heavy wall, but vents are installed at the top and bottom of the Trompe wall so that the heat stored in the wall is transferred to the interior spaces through air movement. Since Felix Tromp used this method for the first time in 1966 in France, this wall is called by this name.

This wall, which is placed at a short distance from the glass, is made of high-density materials such as stone, brick, clay, or greasy gallons of water, and their walls have a dark color. The distance between the glass and the wall should be at least 8 to 10 cm so that the air circulates easily. In the winter season, when the wall vents are open, part of the sun's heat collected in the empty space is transferred to the interior space with the natural flow of air, and in contrast to the cool air of the room, it enters the empty space between the wall and the glass through the lower vent. until it is heated and returned to the interior through the upper vent.

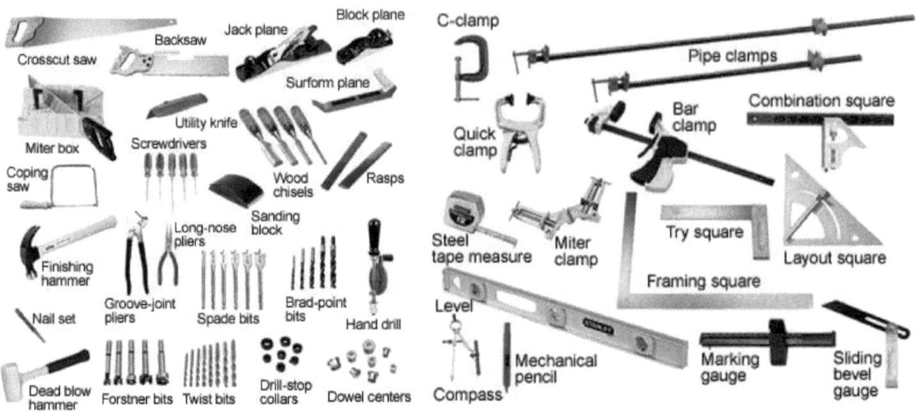

Figure 13. Engineering - Design - Architecture

On cloudy days or on winter nights, the lower and upper openings of the wall should be closed with dampers to prevent the reverse flow of air from the room to the lower space of the wall and glass, and the warm air of the room is not drawn out into the cold space and the cold air does not enter. Do not turn the room.

Atrium: The atrium is a middle space like a central courtyard in the building, which has a transparent and sun-proof roof, and different parts and spaces of the building are formed around the atrium space. Solar heating rays enter the atrium space through the glass roof and in this way (greenhouse phenomenon) thermal energy is stored in the atrium space and enters the interior space through the openings and walls around the atrium, but what is important is to prevent heating. Spaces inside the summer, the space of the atrium should be properly ventilated and its glass roof should be effectively covered with suitable shades.

Glass chambers attached to the building (sunny space): using a heavy wall or a Trumpet wall at the bottom of the sunny space and the back space with upper and lower shutters for movable and external shading for the hot seasons of the year.

Heavy wall: The heavy wall, which has a simple structure, receives the heat of the sun directly and stores it with its high thermal capacity, and then distributes it in the interior space.

Thermosyphon phenomenon: The convective circulation of a fluid that occurs in a closed system, where cold fluid is replaced by hot fluid in the same system, is called thermosyphon. This system is actually a natural displacement cycle. In this system, the energy absorption stage can be connected to the building or completely in a separate environment, and the heat absorbed by the channel is directed to the desired space and in a suitable place, such as a concrete slab or a stone warehouse, which is usually above the absorbing surface. has to be saved.

Glass balconies: Glazing a balcony means covering the balcony with glass, while the balcony is separated from the back room with a glass partition. The glass balcony should have openings to prevent overheating in the summer season. This system is a good system for using the sun's heat for heating in winter.

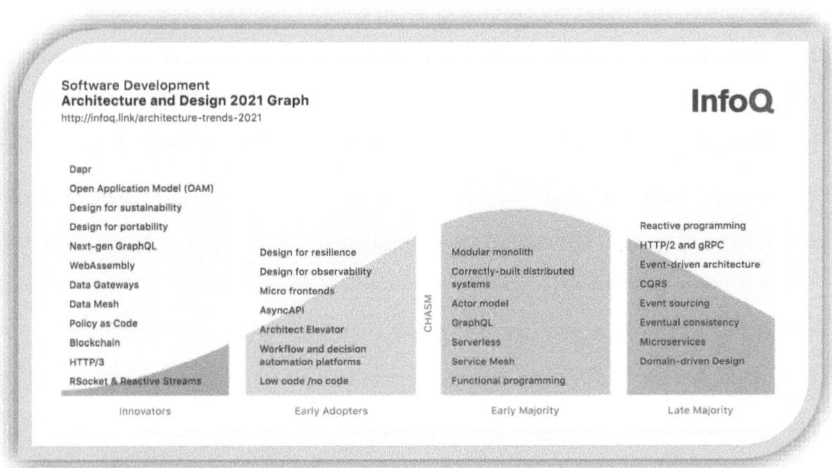

Figure 14. Software Architecture and Design InfoQ Trends Report

Transparent thermal insulation

The passage of heat and air penetration through the building shell is one of the main factors of heat loss in old buildings that need to be renovated. This heat loss can be reduced by using standard windows in the work windows or by sealing the building shell. While these old insulation methods only reduce heat loss, transparent insulation can be used to both prevent heat loss and receive solar energy in heavy building walls such as walls that are thermal mass, raised

Ways to use more solar energy in a passive solar system

❖ The location of the building: suitable sun exposure, the surrounding landscape and the site are very effective in the location of the building. The building should be able to receive sunlight from 9 am to 3 pm in winter. This amount is 90% of solar energy during the above hours. The building should be in the north of the earth and avoid the obstacles that block the sun and its radiation.

❖ Form and orientation of the building: the volume of the building should be able to absorb and penetrate the sun. In the design of the building, one should think about facilitating the solar radiation into the building, and it is better, the volume and length of the building should be east-west. This form is a general factor and has the best result in every climate, but it is more favorable for some other climates. For example, in cold or hot or dry climates, it is better to use compressed forms. Because it reduces the level of contact with the harsh environment and has more freedom of action in moderate climates. Also, in hot and humid climates, the east-west elongated form is better. Layout of spaces to use the sun's heat in this option, heat can be obtained and stored in different ways. For example, it is effective to use materials with high thermal capacity to absorb and store heat in the wall covering or to use large surfaces on the south side to receive the most heat from the sun.

❖ Also, optimal heat acquisition times can be controlled by consumption strategies and placements. For example, eastern facades with large windows increase the heat gain of the building during the morning hours, and shading and low windows on the western facades prevent excess heat from being obtained in the afternoon hours. Layout of spaces to take advantage of the most natural light, using a natural light instead of using electric lights reduces the electrical energy consumption of the building. Ceiling and floor windows and openings and wall windows can be a tool to guide natural light directly or indirectly into the building, which depends on the desired quality of light as well as the performance of the desired space. For example, north and south light have the best qualities, and light from the west side is boring.

Figure 15. A Sustainable Community

❖ Composition of interior spaces: The composition of interior spaces should be such that the spaces get the most solar energy according to their importance. In this sense, by placing the main spaces on the south front, this need can be answered. The southeast and southwest direction can be the answer to the need of the necessary building spaces. Along the north facade, spaces that need less light should be placed, such as garage corridors, etc. East and west views should receive the same amount of light. If it is not possible to use the south light or due to the unfavorable shape of the building, you can use the window on the roof.

❖ The color of the building: the color of the external surfaces is effective on the heat acquired from the sun. Light colors and reflective materials are preferred for warm climates and dark colors and absorbent materials are preferred for cold climates.

❖ Thermal mass of building materials: Higher thermal mass in the case of walls and ceilings increases the heat transfer time between indoor and outdoor spaces. The use of double-walled and triple-walled coverings can make the most of the sun's heat obtained during the day and consumed at night.

❖ Suitable windows: as one of the most influential factors in climate design. The type of material, dimensions and placement of windows will have a significant effect on the heat gained from the sun. Also, the selected type of glass and profile, which today has advanced technology. Although it requires more initial investment, in the long run it reduces the building's energy consumption costs. The following factors cause the least heat loss and the most efficiency of solar energy in the architectural design of the building:

- ✓ It is better to place a building in the front to collect heat from the sun in winter.
- ✓ The materials that make up the outer shell of the building should have the highest thermal resistance. One of them is lightweight concrete.
- ✓ The ratio of the surface of the external shell of the building to the useful volume, the ratio of the roof surface to the useful surface of the building, and the ratio of the surface of the openings in the external shell to the useful surface of the building should be reduced.
- ✓ In summer, planting trees on the west and south-west sides is practically beneficial in order to reduce heat entering the building.
- ✓ Deciduous trees are also good tools and can be planted in the south of the building. Because they have leaves in spring and summer and reduce the amount of radiation of the building, and in winter they are leafless and cannot prevent sunlight from reaching them.
- ✓ Most used living spaces should be designed facing south.
- ✓ Reflective surfaces should be designed on the floors facing the sunny windows, porches and greenhouses connected to empty spaces.

✓ Walls with heavy construction materials should be built in the south face.

✓ Appropriate thermal insulation materials related to thermal resistance should be considered in building construction.

✓ It was intended to increase the efficiency of natural light and reduce the consumption of electrical energy.

✓ The approximate area of the window to use daylight should be 5% of the total floor area of the room.

✓ Windows were placed on the south side of the building, which reduces fuel consumption in winter and lowers the temperature of the building on sunny days.

✓ It becomes necessary to use the canopy, which reduces the energy used to cool the building in the summer.

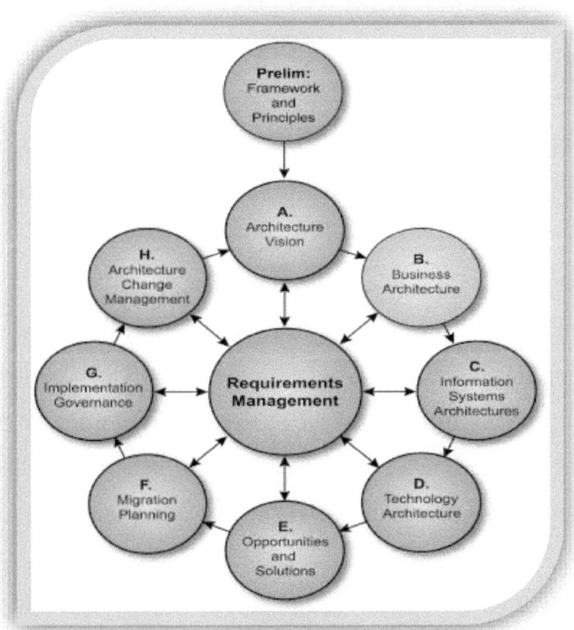

Figure 16. Building Circularity Assessment in the Architecture, Engineering, and Construction Industry: A New Framework

Active solar systems

Active solar systems refer to systems in which other energy, usually electric, is used to transfer the resulting thermal energy to the desired spaces or capacitors or heat exchangers. The electrical energy consuming components are pumps or fans that are placed in the path of heat energy transfer. This method saves a lot on the cost of heating the house and can be easily adapted to the building and is considered a part of the building's rigidity. This system does not have mechanical and electrical components with depreciation and has a long life. Among them, there is no smoke noise and no need for plumbing.

The main types of active solar systems in buildings are:
- ❖ Flat collector with liquid fluid:
- ❖ Flat collector with air fluid:
- ❖ Centralized collector:
- ❖ Heat pump:
- ❖ Solar heat pump:
- ❖ Solar cell (photovoltaic):

Photovoltaic

Photovoltaic history

The term "Photovoltaic" is a combination of the Greek word "Photos" meaning light with "Volt" meaning the production of electricity from light. The discovery of the photovoltaic phenomenon is attributed to the French physicist Edmond becquerel, who in 1839 published his experiments with the wet Cell battery. He observed that the battery voltage did not increase when its silver plates were exposed to sunlight, but the first report of the PV phenomenon in a solid material was in 1877, when two Cambridge scientists R.E. In a paper to the Royal Society, day and W.G. Adams described the changes in the electrical properties of selenium when exposed to light.

Solar cells (photovoltaic)

The main element of photovoltaic technology is the solar cell. Photovoltaic (PV) cells, commonly known as solar cells, are composed of solid-state semiconductor materials. Silicon is the most common semiconductor material used in PV cells due to its abundance. Although silicon is an abundant element and makes up a large percentage of the earth's crust, silicon cells have a high price due to the process of manufacturing and purifying silicon. Photovoltaic cells generate electricity by using sunlight and solar cells and by creating an electrical pressure difference in semiconductors that are properly made. Today, the most effective and cheapest solar cells are a material called silicon. Sand is one of the important sources of silicium, after refining it, silica crystals are obtained and after being cut, it is prepared in the form of plates. In other words, photovoltaic cells, sometimes called solar cells, are made of flakes that convert light directly into electricity.

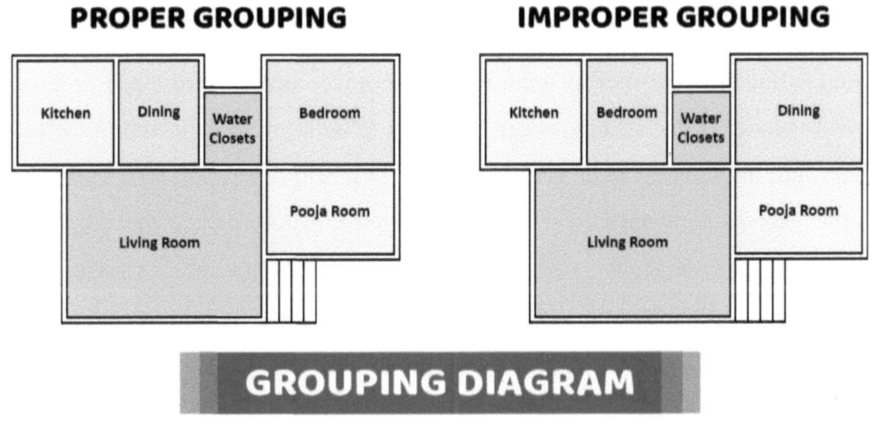

Figure 17 Principles of Building Planning, Designing

Orientation of photovoltaic panels:

The maximum collection of solar radiation occurs when the collector is perpendicular to the direct radiation rays. The best angle for a PV array is basically a function of the time of year when the greatest amount of electricity is needed. Hot climates require the most electricity during the summer for air conditioning, while cold climates require the most electricity in the winter for pumps and fans for heating and lighting systems. Usually, the optimal orientation is towards the south, however, there is a very slight drop in the system up to 20 degrees to the east or west from the south direction. However, the number of daily loads can affect orientation.

Photovoltaic integrated building

Photovoltaic today can be used in existing and new buildings. Its application in building covering is very diverse and opens new ways to creative designers. Due to the fact that the power source of photovoltaic cells is sunlight, therefore, the location of the cells is the walls of the building that have a suitable field for direct sunlight. Therefore, the place of use of photovoltaic tiles is often the external facades and external surfaces of the roof of the building. Photovoltaic cells are made in glass of different colors, so that architects can use them in addition to their main function to beautify buildings. These cells have the ability to transmit between 80% and 90% of sunlight. This quality makes the windows equipped with solar cells help to keep the air inside the house cool in the summer and in addition to beautifying the facade of the building, provide the required electricity.

Facades of the building

Facades occupy the majority of the surface of the shell of a building. In fact, a facade conveys the first visual feeling of the building to its viewers, and the architects use the facade to express ideas and translate the client's wishes with a special language of shape and color. Standard photovoltaic modules can be attached to the existing wall of the building to provide an aesthetically successful appearance.

These units are connected to the structure without the need for insulation, which is done by grid infrastructure in photovoltaic modules. Therefore, photovoltaic systems can be considered as an important part of building facade elements. The main face of a photovoltaic layer as a covering material is similar to a colored glass. Photovoltaic layers provide long-term protection against atmospheric conditions and can be cut and prepared in any size, shape, design and color, and even bring part of the daylight into the building. These building elements can act as simple facade panels, multi-functional elements for cold and warm facades, as a shading or opening system.

Figure 18. A house with a green neighborhood Project

Semi-transparent facades

Photovoltaic sheets, like windows, can perform their function of transparency and back view in two ways. Photovoltaic cell alone can be very fine or laser and thus provide 20 to 50% filtered vision. Semi-transparent non-crystalline silicon modules are specially prepared for this function. On the other hand, in a similar way, crystalline cells can light up the interior while creating a vision filter. Even by adding layers of glass to the main unit of semi-transparent photovoltaic, heat and sound insulation is also provided for the special needs of the building.

Figure 19. 10 Architecture Projects Made Possible by Engineers

Canopy systems

In today's architecture, there is a strong need for shading systems in the building market, which leads to the wide use of large openings and curtains or other canopies. In the meantime, photovoltaics with different shapes can be used as canopies above the windows or part of the roof structure, provided that the use of these canopies does not lead to imposing an additional load on the building structure. Photovoltaic shading systems can be arranged in such a way and in a direction that they can be used both to produce the most energy and to provide varying degrees of shade.

Roof materials

Roofs are ideal for photovoltaics. Because usually the shading factors on the roof are much less than the ground level and usually the roof provides a large unused surface for this purpose. An ideal sloping roof for photovoltaics is a south-facing roof with an angle equal to ±15 degrees of latitude for the best energy production. In this regard, southeast and southwest facing roofs are also acceptable. Photovoltaic panels can be easily installed on the roof of existing buildings. A beautiful way to use photovoltaics on the roof of a building is to use PV tiles or tuffals, which allows them to be easily installed by a roofing contractor, like tiles or other roof coverings. Flat roofs also have advantages such as convenient access and easy installation.

The classic method in this regard is the arrangement and arrangement of photovoltaic units on its network infrastructure and then installing them on the roof. In this method, in addition to paying special attention to the arrangement of the modules and their installation, which is also done on the sloping roof, necessary precautions should also be taken regarding the wind force.

Recent experiences and developments in this field have made these systems lighter, easier and faster to use. Ideally, sloping roofs are the best option for installing panels. Gable roofs are better than flat roofs, because the parts of the roof facing north can be used to let light into the space, while the southern surface of the gables can be a place to install photovoltaics. Covering with photovoltaics on the south surface can also be done using semi-transparent panels that both allow light to enter the space and generate electricity. If the panels are designed along with the body of the roof, pieces in the form of curved pottery or tiles can be used.

Advantages of using photovoltaic systems
- ✓ Photovoltaic technology is mature, robust and reliable, has no moving parts and requires little maintenance.
- ✓ It does not require fuel or a fuel supply network.
- ✓ Installing a photovoltaic system is relatively easy and quick, especially for grid-connected systems.
- ✓ The components used in photovoltaic systems have proven their reliability during long-term use.
- ✓ They are resistant to ultraviolet rays, weather and high temperature.
- ✓ They are modular and the systems can exist in any size.
- ✓ A stand-alone photovoltaic system can provide power almost anywhere on the planet.

✓ Photovoltaic system reduces greenhouse gas and carbon dioxide emissions.

✓ Photovoltaic systems generally reduce pollution.

✓ Photovoltaic system helps to conserve scarce resources.

Figure 20. 5 Pioneering Female Architects

Solar cells

The first device and the smallest independent unit of photovoltaic systems is the solar cell. The size of solar cells is several millimeters. For example, calculators, wristwatches up to 10 x 10 cm. Today, the most effective solar cells are made of a material called silicon, and sand is one of the important sources of silicon. Although silicon is an abundant element and constitutes a large percentage of the earth's crust, it has a high price due to the special process and purification of silicon.

Modules

The primary structure of solar collectors in photovoltaic systems are modules. Each photovoltaic module consists of a number of solar cells that are electrically connected to each other and are embedded and protected in a supporting frame. PV modules often have a glass sheet on the front to allow light to pass through. While thin semiconductor layers protect it from wind, rain and hail storms. Currently, silicon-type modules are manufactured in different voltages and currents from 200-800 cm2.

Arrays

Photovoltaic arrays are: photovoltaic modules and its support frame on which the module is mounted electrically and mechanically. The design of arrays is done in two ways: one is flat arrays in which solar cells are connected to each other using suitable and usually non-fragile materials, and the other is concentrator arrays in which using appropriate methods such as lenses, mirrors, etc., the rays are focused on the cells.

Regulators and controllers

Regulators and controllers are equipment that adjust the battery voltage and control the electric current entering the battery. They also prevent possible damage to the battery. The purpose of their installation is to prevent overcharging of batteries and disconnection to drain the battery at night.

Converter

Considering that the electricity produced by the photovoltaic arrays is DC direct current, so it is necessary to convert the said output into alternating and standard AC current with the appropriate voltage and phase and frequency to connect to the power grid. The preparation and conversion of electricity is done by a device called a converter (inverter).

K) Photovoltaic systems integrated in architecture are available in the following forms:
- ✓ Classic framed modules.
- ✓ Flexible crystal transparent modules.
- ✓ Thin film modules with solar cells.
- ✓ Roof tiles with solar cells.
- ✓ Modules with colored solar cells.
- ✓ Translucent modules with tiny holes.

Solar systems based on facade are:

- ✓ Curtain wall system.
- ✓ Rain curtain cover system.
- ✓ Fixed shades.
- ✓ Movable shades.
- ✓ Retaining wall with sloping panels.
- ✓ steep wall.

Figure 21. 7 Chicagoland Neighborhoods for Architecture Lovers

Photovoltaic systems integrated with the building

At first, photovoltaic systems were used separately in the building, the most common of which was placing solar panels on the roof, until now, in 1994, solar architecture was formed for the first time in Japan. In the beginning, it was tried to use solar panels according to the local aesthetics and architecture, until today they reached a place where solar cells are referred to as a material. Nowadays, the use of photovoltaic systems has become very important and attractive among designers and architects. Therefore, these buildings should be built in a correct way and with a suitable design that does not cause problems for the photovoltaic system itself or for the building after installation. Based on this, in order to avoid architectural contamination, it is necessary to consider photovoltaic systems as a self-defined design or an architectural element, so that photovoltaics become a known part of the building and completely integrated with it during the design process. Just as in the design of building elements such as walls, windows and awnings, attention is paid to the geographical latitude of the place and climate, neighborhoods, coordination with passive solar systems, sizes, directions, angles and other things, photovoltaics are also in the status of building elements is related to these issues.

Therefore, in the design and combination of photovoltaics with the building, attention should be paid to all the things that an architect designer goes through during the design process of various factors. The purpose of this treatise is to describe the methods of using photovoltaics in buildings.

Determining the optimal direction and slope of photovoltaic panels

With the increase in the intensity of the sun's rays, the output of the photovoltaic system also increases. Therefore, the power efficiency of the photovoltaic system has a direct relationship with the amount of solar energy received. On the other hand, the change in the angle of the sun's radiation and the amount of radiation at different times during the day also affects the production of photovoltaic power.

Therefore, the efficiency of the photovoltaic system depends on the direction and slope of the installed panels in relation to the sun's radiation, and as a result, the orientation and slope of the photovoltaic panels is affected by the amount of solar energy received. The amount of receiving solar energy in different places is different based on the difference in geographical latitude, height above sea level, atmospheric phenomena.

For this reason, in order to obtain information about the radiation, the meteorological station, the geographical latitude and altitude of that place should be determined so that the average monthly and annual radiation received from the sun can be determined at the level of the horizon and all levels with different directions and slopes for the desired place. One of the methods that is used to find the right direction and slope of photovoltaic panels in the world is to use actions. In this method, based on meteorological data of direct and scattered solar radiation and using computer programs, the amount of solar radiation on all horizontal and vertical surfaces in different directions and slopes is drawn monthly or annually.

If the photovoltaic panels are placed according to the angle of each of these slopes, they will have different efficiency based on the amount of energy they receive from the sun. Based on this, it is possible to determine the optimal directions and tilt angles of photovoltaic panels.

The maximum point in this action is the place that receives the most amount of energy from the sun throughout the year. Because the more vertical the sun shines on a surface, the more energy will reach that surface. As a result, if a photovoltaic panel is placed in this direction and angle of inclination, it will produce maximum electricity energy. Therefore, the orientation of photovoltaic panels is an important issue, but determining its angle does not require much accuracy.

Figure 22. Pu'er Shan Zhi Meng Custom-Designed Neighborhood

Because a little difference in deviation from the optimal direction will not cause problems, but the angle of inclination of the panels relative to the horizon is a more important issue. By determining the optimal tilt angle, depending on the time of using the system, about 95% of the maximum output energy can be obtained.

The effect of shadows on photovoltaic panels

Shade is one of the factors that affect the amount of access to the sun. The reflection of the ground, the shadow of the surrounding buildings, the shadow of the building itself and the shadow of the panels on each other may affect the photovoltaic system. The architect must design the position and location of the photovoltaic panels in such a way that there is no shadow effect on them. This is because the shadow on the photovoltaic cells will cause damage to the cells in addition to the reduction or lack of efficiency. Therefore, in the design of such a building, it is necessary to pay attention to the issue of shading from the beginning and to carry out a detailed analysis of the shadow before the photovoltaic system is combined with the building in order to obtain the maximum electricity production.

Shading of the building itself, neighborhoods and obstacles

- ✓ Shading between buildings should be avoided. Building density is an interesting area. In dense spaces such as urban centers, the distance between buildings is limited. Therefore, facade systems are more sensitive to shading, and in comparison, with roof systems, more distances are needed between buildings.
- ✓ Shading due to architectural forms should be avoided. The distance between the photovoltaic roofs and other objects should be such that it does not create a continuous shadow.
- ✓ Where shading is unavoidable, careful selection of components and the shape and position of panels reduces power loss.

Figure 23. Gentrification's Effect on Urban Communities

Shading of trees

The shade of vegetation may also have an inappropriate effect on photovoltaic systems. Therefore, as much as possible in the landscape design, plants and trees should be planted in a direction that does not block the sun's rays to the panels, or shorter shrubs with limited growth should be used. Planning in this field is important to prevent shading problems in the years after building construction and tree growth. Therefore, in the northern hemisphere, it is better to plant trees in the north and in the southern hemisphere in the south of the building, and according to the height of the building, trees with limited growth should be used.

Shading of the cloudy sky

Cloudy environments also cast a shadow on the photovoltaic panels, and due to the reduction of the sun's rays and the reduction of the brightness of the light from the cloudy sky, the output of the photovoltaics is reduced.

Coordination between photovoltaic systems and passive solar systems in the building

Designers usually consider solar design as a limitation rather than an opportunity. If the architect designs the building according to the climatic conditions of the place and in accordance with passive solar systems, the conditions of that building will be close to the comfort limit of the residents, and if he combines the photovoltaic system, which is an active solar system, with the building in a suitable way, the result better work and building energy efficiency will be much higher. In this way, he can bring the micro-climatic conditions of the building closer to the limit of comfort and turn it into a self-sufficient building.

In the design, it should be noted that the use of photovoltaic systems does not conflict with the use of passive solar systems, and both systems are perfectly coordinated by designers in order to reduce energy consumption, but if the photovoltaic system is properly combined in the building envelope, it is possible to prevent penetration It caught the sun and produced the electricity needed for cooling. Designers can integrate photovoltaic systems with the building in such a way that the possibility of ventilation, the use of the sun's heat in winter, the use of natural light, the view to the outside and other things are provided together.

The result is that the best efficiency is achieved when the active and passive solar systems in a building are coordinated and adapted. To achieve this goal, the overall energy solution for the building must be predicted before starting the design process.

Ventilation of photovoltaic systems

Ventilation of photovoltaic systems as the temperature increases, the output power from the cells decreases and as a result, the efficiency of photovoltaic panels decreases. Therefore, in the combination of photovoltaics with the building, attention should be paid to the issue of their natural or mechanical ventilation in the design process so that they reach a lower temperature and continue their optimal efficiency.

Methods of combining photovoltaic systems with buildings

Methods of combining photovoltaic systems with buildings photovoltaic systems can be integrated and integrated in buildings with roofs, skylights, atriums, facades, canopies, etc.

Figure 24. Pu'er Shan Zhi Meng Custom-Designed Neighborhood

Photovoltaic systems integrated with the roof

Photovoltaic panels on flat roofs can be combined in the form of flexible thin film cells and on sloping roofs in the form of photovoltaic tiles. Also, they can be used as a building shell with a sloping roof system or connected to the roof structure. The level of combination and directness of photovoltaic elements should be compatible with any other non-photovoltaic elements in order to combine structural and aesthetic issues in architecture and obtain a conscious and architectural product.

Also, in the design of roof systems, the issue of snow accumulation and moisture removal is important. For this purpose, you should choose appropriate solutions in accordance with the climate conditions of the place to remove rainwater and snow accumulation on the photovoltaic panels.

Photovoltaic systems integrated with skylights and atriums

In this type of building, to combine photovoltaics with the roof, the architect can design the roof as integrated skylights with photovoltaics. Also, semi-transparent photovoltaic panels can replace the glass of ceiling windows and atriums, which the creative and experienced designer uses the quality of light in the form of spots. The building designer can integrate photovoltaics with atriums, so that opaque or semi-transparent photovoltaics are placed on the side facing the sun and transparent glass behind them. In this way, photovoltaics prevents direct sunlight from entering the interior space and at the same time generate electricity from the sun's rays.

Photovoltaic systems integrated with the façade

There are different ways to combine photovoltaic systems with the facade, each of which can be proposed in the design process depending on the type of design and the choice of designers, and the best option can be used according to the conditions of the building. In facade systems, it is possible to combine opaque, semi-transparent and glass panels side by side in a vertical or staggered manner so that each natural light enters the interior as much as necessary and photovoltaic panels produce electricity. Also, prevent unwanted sunlight from entering the space during hot weather.

Photovoltaic systems integrated with canopies

Opaque photovoltaic panels, in combination with the building or the light shelf, protect the windows, louvres, installation and interior space from the direct rays of the sun, and at the same time, the light entry conditions They provide scattered and indirect light into the space. Photovoltaic canopies can be placed horizontally, inclined or bridges on the vertical wall. The advantage of photovoltaic canopies compared to other canopies or curtains is that, in addition to preventing heat from entering the building and reducing the load on cooling devices, it also produces the electricity required by cooling systems.

Determining the type and power of the photovoltaic system

The type of a photovoltaic system depends on conditions such as the type of loads connected to the AC or DC system or both, the presence or absence of an auxiliary power generator, connection or non-connection to the local or national network and how it is connected. The network is unidirectional or bidirectional. Before designing, one should first decide whether the independent photovoltaic system is self-supporting, or connected to the city power grid. Independent systems need special batteries to store electricity, and their electricity production is lower than systems connected to the grid, and often in remote locations from the power grid is used. If the photovoltaic system is connected to the city grid, there will be a guarantee of electricity supply. Because electricity is exchanged between the system and the network, and the network acts as unlimited storage.

Figure 25. Neighborhood

Battery-powered systems also require battery maintenance, but unlike network-connected systems, they do not require special maintenance. Of course, in deciding on the type of system, the battery and maintenance costs should be considered and based on the needs and type of life, determine what type of system will be more suitable. The power of a photovoltaic system is defined as the maximum direct current efficiency of the solar system in kilowatts. Therefore, a 2-kW system, when fully exposed to the sun's rays, produces 2000 W of DC electricity, and then this direct current is converted to usable AC alternating current through a converter, and its output is 1.7 kW. decreases.

The power of photovoltaic systems depends on these things: the amount of electric load consumed and personal needs, the location of the system and the climate of sunlight and the area of the space available on the roof or facade, but the most important limitation for the power of the photovoltaic system is the available budget. In addition to affecting the architecture and its design, this system also challenges those involved in the planning and design process, i.e., architects and other engineers, to develop their innovative solutions for the integration of the building support system with the provided photovoltaic power.

Architects and engineers who work with each other are asked to integrate photovoltaics into at least four levels of integration during building planning and design:

- ❖ Designing a building (shape, size, orientation, color).
- ❖ Mechanical integrity (multifunctionality of a photovoltaic element).
- ❖ Electrical integrity (connected to the grid or direct use of electricity).
- ❖ The system should be integrated with normal building care and maintenance.

Building design requirements with photovoltaic cells

Considering that electricity consumption in Iran is increasing every year and a large amount of the country's energy is used in the form of electricity in the building sector, and also considering the increasing need for energy sources and decreasing Fossil energy sources and dams, the limitations of electricity supply and fuel supply for remote points and attention to reducing air pollution, hence the use of solar energy to generate electricity in Iran, which will allow the sun's rays to reach Manatan and Asra. It requires power and power, it is from solar energy, it seems necessary that with the advancement of technology and the need to save energy, today's world is moving towards the integration of more and more photovoltaic systems.

Many of these are seen in different countries, which are progressing day by day. For example, photovoltaics is combined with the building as a construction element or material, and in addition to the advantages that they have on their own, when combined with architecture, their benefits are multiplied and they will no longer be just energy producers.

Today, architects are rapidly moving towards combining photovoltaics with buildings and replacing them with building materials, which is one of the fastest growing sectors of the construction industry, and this technique is well known and used in Europe and America. Life is supported. It should be said about the economic issues of this system: that most of the expenses are related to the initial costs of its production. It will be less than the price of electricity in the city grid, and when our oil and electricity find their true value and the use of photovoltaic electricity costs the same as the electricity of the national grid in one-month, solar energy and solar energy will be yours. One of the components of any place to use photovoltaics is its sunlight condition. In this sense, Tehran city has been compared with some European cities in terms of sunlight.

Figure 26. BRONZEVILLE, The City of Neighborhoods

The state of sunshine in Iran and the sky of Tehran

The country of Iran is located between 25° and 10° to 39° and 25° north latitude, while European countries are located between 40° to 70° latitude, the United States of America is located between 30° to 50° latitude, and Canada is located between 50° to 50° latitude. are Iran is located in the middle of this latitude and is closer to the equator and as we know, in the areas near the equator, the sun's rays are perpendicular to the earth's surface, and in the areas near the two poles, the sun's rays are more inclined. It is an increase. It shows a great difference.

However, in these European cities with few solar hours, there are a large number of integrated buildings with photovoltaics, which are very good examples of the effectiveness of this system in the world. The country of Iran is full of solar energy in order to have cities with more than 3000 hours of sunshine per year and it only needs a national planning to use this energy. Due to the fact that the approach to photovoltaics is growing and successful in the world and is justified from the scientific and economic point of view, it is widely used in different countries.

Design requirements

In order to properly integrate photovoltaics with the building, they should be considered from the beginning of the design process as a part of the basic design of the building and in accordance with the architect's plan. In order to achieve this goal, it is necessary to pay attention to various issues related to photovoltaics and building, as well as the effect they have on each other, during the design. Because when the photovoltaics are combined with the building.

In addition to electricity generation, they are also related to the appearance, roof, elements and other systems and even the environment around the building. Therefore, it is necessary to examine this issue in the design process from different aspects and to find an appropriate and coordinated solution with other factors. Some of the design needs are general, that is, they can be the same everywhere, and the designers and building engineers, knowing their principles, regulations, and strategies, can design them anywhere according to the type of design and issues related to the wall. provide a design process, but some other design needs of these buildings should be considered for the city and specially coordinated with the information and conditions of that place.

Figure 27. Neighborhoods of Santiago: Walking the Capital's Best Spots - Chile Travel

In this section, the design requirements are briefly introduced:
- ✓ The effect of climatic factors on photovoltaic panels.
- ✓ Determining the optimal direction and slope of photovoltaic panels.
- ✓ The effect of shade sizes on the arrangement, composition and spacing of photovoltaic panels.
- ✓ Coordination between photovoltaic systems and passive solar systems in the building.
- ✓ Ventilation of photovoltaic systems integrated with the building.
- ✓ The methods of combining photovoltaic systems with the building, in which photovoltaics can be integrated with the roof, roof windows and atriums, its elements and canopies.
- ✓ Replacing photovoltaics with regular building materials.
- ✓ The effect of the building plan on the power of the photovoltaic system.

- ✓ The effect of the slope of the facade of the building on the power of the photovoltaic system.
- ✓ Determining the type and power of the photovoltaic system integrated with the building.
- ✓ The effect of the need for cooling or heating on the angle of inclination of photovoltaic panels.
- ✓ The effect of building performance on the location and angle of the photovoltaic panels.
- ✓ Coordination between the architect and other engineers in the building design.

Indigenous ways of designing integral buildings with photovoltaics

As it was said, one of the goals of this treatise is to provide a solution for the factors that influence the design process of such buildings. For this purpose, in the continuation of the design methods of integrated buildings with photovoltaics in the city of Tehran according to its local needs, the necessary suggestions and solutions have been examined.

The effect of climatic factors

Climatic and geographical factors can affect or even reduce the power production of photovoltaic systems. Therefore, when photovoltaics is combined with buildings, the effect of climatic issues related to architecture in these systems should also be predicted in order to reach the desired result.

The ambient temperature has a great effect on the efficiency of photovoltaic systems, so that with the increase in temperature, the production power of the cell decreases and with the decrease in temperature, the voltage increases. In the city of Tehran, during the hot months, especially at noon, the air temperature reaches above 25 degrees, and this temperature reduces the efficiency of photovoltaics, which is necessary, to design with appropriate measures to avoid the heat of the panels and the bottom of the roof. Natural or mechanical ventilation will increase the efficiency of the system.

Strategy

In dual view systems, by creating an opening, you can use the wind and natural ventilation in the building to ventilate the back of the photovoltaic panels and increase their efficiency. slow down according to the diagram of the temperature and temperature of the day, we can see that in the past years, the need for heating was more in Tehran, but in recent years, the temperature of the temperature is decreasing and the temperature of the temperature is increasing.

Therefore, the need for cooling should be taken into consideration and appropriate measures should be taken for the hot months. Considering the need for more electricity in these months, this issue can affect the design and slope of the photovoltaic panels, which will be investigated further.

Figure 28. The World's Most Creative Neighborhoods

Chapter III

Introduction of domestic and foreign samples

Internal samples

Abgineh Museum: Tehran's Abgineh and Pottery Museum is one of the most beautiful and exquisite museums in Iran. The main palace of the museum and its adjacent buildings are valuable buildings of the late 13th century and have many characteristics of the buildings of the Qajar era. The said building was built about 85 years ago for one of the officials of the Qajar period named Ahmad Qawam nicknamed Qawam al-Sultaneh and it was used by him until 1954. After him, the building was handed over to the Egyptian embassy for 7 years. It was taken over by the Commercial Bank for a while, and finally in 1957, the building was sold to Farah Diba's office, and after major repairs, it was decided to create a museum in it.

The transformation of the building with museum equipment was done by three groups of Iranian, Austrian and German engineers under the supervision of Austrian architect Hans Hollein. The museum building with an area of 1040 square meters is located in a garden of 7200 square meters. The design of the building is octagonal and false columns are built in its entrance. The building has two floors and a basement. The ground floor is connected to the upper floor through a two-way wooden staircase in the style of Russian architecture.

The foyer of the museum, which was built in the shape of a dome before the establishment of the Egyptian embassy in this place, was flattened by the Egyptians. The basement of the building, which is now the location of the museum's library, has the atmosphere of traditional Iranian architecture. This library contains 2000 volumes of books in English and 1100 volumes of books in Persian in the fields of cinema, theater, architecture, painting, music, photography, art history and archeology, which are used by the public.

The widespread use of doors and windows with various arrangements in traditional Iranian architecture has led the architect to use double windows instead of porches. In this way, behind the glass windows, there are wooden doors that make it possible to adjust the light and heat inside the building. The general architectural style of this building, like many buildings of the Qajar period, is a combination of traditional Iranian architecture and 19th century European architecture.

The National Museum of Ancient Iran: The National Museum of Iran, which is about 60 years old, is not only the largest museum of archeology and history in Iran, but it is also considered one of the world's largest museums in terms of the variety and quality of its works. This museum is called as mother museum in the culture of Iranian museum owners. This building aims to preserve and research the works of the past, to introduce and display and transfer their heritage to future generations, to create and strengthen understanding between ethnic groups and nations, to recognize and display their contribution to world culture and civilization, to help and strive to improve and increase the amount of knowledge.

Figure 29. 18 Best Neighborhoods in Chicago for 2023 (By a Local)

The general public, especially the researchers, has been established. The first museum was established in 1917 solar called the national museum or the museum of education in one of the large rooms of the Ministry of Education located on the north side of the Dar al-Funun building. This museum had 270 objects of bronze, clay, glass, coins, old weapons, seals, wooden objects, patches, books and textiles, which were collected by the employees of the antiquities department or donated by the people.

Since the plan and map of a museum is in harmony with the subject and objects inside it and is connected and continuous with the history and art of that land, Andre Godard tried to display Iranian Sasanian architecture in the museum building. Most of the works of that time were the ancient objects of old Iran and reminiscent of Sassanid architecture. From this point of view, the facade and the entrance of the museum were built in the style of the facade of Ivan Madaen (Kasari arch).

For this reason, the color of the bricks was determined to be dark red to represent the architecture of the Sassanid era. The building includes two museums in two separate buildings, namely the museum of ancient Iran, founded in 1938 AH and the museum of the Islamic period, founded in 1997.

The museum building is actually a rectangular cube that consists of three parts. Its entrance is made through a large Sassanid arch, which is reminiscent of the Sassanid palaces, especially in Firozabad, Fars, and expresses itself majestically in the urban complex. The rectangular volume of the museum has dimensions of 34 x 100 meters and consists of three entrance parts, the object displays area and the office space, which is moderated by breaks in its long side view.

The main hall of the museum is designed with a length of 61 meters and a width of 34 meters, and it has an internal skylight with dimensions of 16 x 16 meters, which provides adequate light to the main space of the hall. In the eastern and western side walls, there are tall and narrow windows that create a uniform and repetitive rhythm along the hall.

This hall continues on two floors that are connected to each other through a large staircase. The administrative section has a U-shaped plan, which is located along the north side of the main hall. This section has a separate entrance and has four floors. The building is placed on a platform of carved white travertine stone at a height of 1.5 meters from the street level, and the same white stone in the form of a thick cornice, which is the top of the building, defines the end point of the roof. The brickwork of the external walls continues from this platform to the roof cornice. Above the stone cornice, a brick parapet completes the 12-meter-high building.

Museum of Holy Defense: Museum of holy defense and promoting the culture of resistance as a place to present a small part of the saga of the zealous Iranian nation during the revolution and holy defense, along with the large cultural collections of the city, such as the Tehran book garden, the national library, the Islamic republic, garden of art, Tehran, Quran house and great mosque of Tehran are placed as the cultural hub of Tehran. In this collection, you can see the presentation of the content, the epic spirit and the teachings of the holy defense in the form of modern technologies, including demonstration, interactive and integrated.

The halls are equipped with information kiosks with the possibility of touch screens to receive accurate information related to the oral history of the holy defense era, documented by the speeches of the commanders of the eight years of the holy defense, as well as valid national and international documents, and have a fun and exciting atmosphere 18 A hectare with special facilities for entertaining and spending leisure time of visitors.

This museum includes numerous exhibitions of art and cultural works related to the holy defense, which are organized by using intelligent surveillance systems and using a well-equipped and high-capacity database to store and maintain the information and documents of the holy defense, including photos, videos, and multimedia. Documents and documents are maps. In this complex, Khorramshahr grand mosque has been built in real dimensions as a symbol of the resistance of noble people of Islamic Iran. In all open and closed spaces, special arrangements have been made for the passage of veterans and disabled people.

There are three amphitheaters with facilities and programs:

- ✓ Persian Gulf Amphitheater: with a capacity of 500 seats, the possibility of holding shows, conferences and cultural and artistic programs and simultaneous translation facilities, Dolby and Serand sound, the possibility of showing digital 3D movies with special glasses.
- ✓ Hoize amphitheater: with a capacity of 120 seats, the possibility of holding conferences and specialized and educational courses.

✓ Rosengard amphitheater: in the open air with a capacity of 700 seats and the possibility of holding various cultural and artistic programs.

Figure 30. Seattle's Best Historic Neighborhoods

The use of artworks by Iranian artists by reconstructing a part of different approaches to holy defense including:

✓ Part of a neighborhood in Khorramshahr city.

✓ Part of Abadan refinery using original parts.

✓ Warriors' strongholds in the cold and hot climates of the fronts and rebuilding the presence of Islamic warriors in these strongholds.

✓ The existence of a specialized bookstore of holy defense with more than eleven thousand book titles and equipping it as an electronic bookstore of holy defense.

✓ The possibility of maintaining a memorial of 240 thousand honorable martyrs of the holy defense and their permanent display in the Hall of butterflies.

✓ Commemorating and showing the dimensions of life and epics of martyred commanders and witnesses of the holy defense in prawned Hall, creating a place for permanent meetings of the veterans of the holy defense.

Foreign samples

Fort Worth Art Museum: The Fort Worth museum of modern art in texas and next to the Kimble Art Museum, Louis Kahn's outstanding work is the largest modern art museum in America after new York's Mooder, and it is considered one of Tadao Ando's greatest foreign works. All the structural signs of his design can be seen in this museum. The undisturbed volumes consist of simple geometric surfaces in a bed of clear modulation with primary materials such as exposed concrete, wood glass and light that slowly shines on them and displays continuous reflection with the help of water, in order to create a calm and minimalist atmosphere. They are recruited with human feelings.

The museum consists of several rectangular cubes that are combined in an L-shaped plan and thus includes a reflecting pool. As the building is fragmented, a set of rectangular cube volumes is displayed. This is Louis Kahn's solution for the Kimble art Museum. Ando has tried to give a positive response to the nearby valuable work. On the other hand, the linear form has opened the possibility of conceptual and physical expansion of the building. The walls of the site have the task of delaying the perception of the building by the audience.

First, exhibition spaces and galleries that are formed between concrete walls. Then, a space between the galleries and a transparent glass wall, sometimes with stairs and sometimes with a space with walls from the ceiling to the glass floor, is used to see the distant view of the city on the other side of the pool, and finally, an area beyond the glass walls with a ceiling cantilevered consists of a Y-shaped element that supports the roof that prevents the direct sunlight on the artworks and mixes from below with the water that goes up to the adjacent glass wall of the building, all arrangements that Ando Its intermediary has been able to place the museum in a glass cover, unlike many other museums.

San Francisco Museum of modern art: The museum building is located in a piece of land surrounded by three tall buildings, and for this reason, it required a special and strong image, which at the same time cannot be compared with the neighboring buildings. The staircase facade of the building is brick in front and contains a series of exhibition spaces, all of which receive light from above.

Despite the unfavorable ratio of 1 to 4 plots and the entire built surface, natural light has been considered. Creating an integrated interior space, creating an external shell that, contrary to the characteristics of the facade, makes the building appear unknown and invites passers-by inside. The facade is opened in the center and reveals the presence of a cylindrical volume decorated with two-color marble. This iconic shape is cut at a steep angle at the top, directing light into the central cavity of the building, around which are the access ways to the theaters.

3GATTI Car Museum: The car test was a subject, for the design of a structure that is only dedicated to the car. Because the car is a design, a new discovery, a field of learning, the subject of articles and a means of transportation. Here, the structure is the intersection of cars and humans in an organic structural space that has an open space with a large scale.

There are no stairs, walls, floors and elevators here, but you are dealing with sloping surfaces and climbing to the upper floors is accompanied by a fluid movement. The structure is based on a sloping ramp whose entrance and exit are separated by a glass partition. The topology of the building is as if the visitor has the status of a spectator watching a movie whose main actor is a car and the frame should be the witness of the movie. The facade of the building is such that its use can be recognized from the surrounding streets for passing cars and from the eyes of air travelers or even internet users who look through a satellite view.

Denver Art Museum: The development plan of the Denver art Museum is actually an extension of the existing museum building, which was designed by the Italian architect Gio Ponti. The importance of vitality and growth or modernization that ruled over the city of Denver. The new building was localized and to display modern and contemporary art as well as a collection of African and Oceanic art. The new building was the result of a joint venture between the Davis Architects Group in collaboration with the Mortensen company.

Figure 31. Inside Moscow's 'Golden Mile,' Where Homes Sell for $2 Million and up

To complete the vision of the extension, Daniel Libeskind's design studio worked closely with other teams involved in the project and with the client. The result is a closely related building that has become a major cultural landmark in Denver and has attracted thousands of visitors to the museum complex since its opening. The new building is functionally and aesthetically closely related to the existing building of Ponti museum, community center and library. The new building itself has an urban centrality to the project, not designed as a single building, but as part of a series of historic public spaces and gateways in this developing part of the city. The materials used in the building belong to the present time, for example, the use of titanium sheets in the facade, and this modernization has linked the traditional part of the city of Denver to the 21st century. The close connection and response to a large range of lighting variations, coloring, spatial effects, temperature and weather conditions have been one of the challenges of the Denver art museum building. The new building was not formed solely based on a specific thought and to respond to an idea and thought, and also its formation is in a way that does not completely separate the outside and inside space and the two are fluidly connected.   Therefore, visiting it will give a person a new sensory experience. The integration of all the mentioned issues in this building inspires a kind of respect.

B5) Maxi national museum: The exterior of the Maxi Museum reminds one of the works of Frank Gehry, a famous contemporary architect. The same boldness in showing strange spaces and the same effect they have in making the city more beautiful. This building with its colorful facade is part of an addition to a 19th century school. The colors of the facade are taken directly from the surroundings and the bricks of the old school building, the sky, the trees and plants of the playground lend their colors to this new building. The windows of this building are very small, like the other parts of the facade, but instead, there are a lot of them, which makes enough light to enter the interior and illuminate it completely. When large windows are used for more light, the view outside easily distracts the students, but nothing happens.

Figure 32. Inside Moscow's 'Golden Mile,' Where Homes Sell for $2 Million and up

Chapter IV

Village Design

Introduction

A look at the stages of historical development of many cities in our country leads us to the fact that although urban development in them was accompanied by quantitative development of the city and an increase in construction along with an increase in urban incomes, but in terms of environmental quality, this development has been associated with many challenges. One of the constant problems of our country's cities today is the lack of recreational and tourism spaces.

Figure 33. Village

Tourism has become a basis for idea generation, entertainment, job creation and entrepreneurship, and in a more modern form has become an interconnected network of economic, social, civil and cultural infrastructures, while the vast country of Iran, with its extensive cultural, heritage and natural attractions, it is one of the top countries in the world in terms of tourist attractions and has many potentials for the development of tourism, tourism and leisure industry at the national and international levels.

Mazandaran province with many pristine and natural areas and many God-given blessings and unique climate in the country, and proximity to the Caspian Sea and its Alborz slopes, including the most innovative and fun tourist areas in the country and even Iran is a neighboring country and the annual return of millions of travelers to this province shows the high position of this province in the tourism system of the country and the amount of attention of compatriots to this province and its capabilities.

The site of this project, located in Amol city and also located near Haraz river, all the capabilities and potentials of the green region of Mazandaran, including the benefit of favorable climate, greenery and vegetation density, proximity to the Caspian Sea, welcome travelers and ...

Generalities

Problem statement

Proper response to the physical, mental and spiritual needs of human beings is one of the necessities that public spaces should be organized in the form of various and specific functions in this direction. Lack or weakness of social functions in this regard leads to inefficiency in human beings and its negative consequences will affect the community. The growth and development of urban life and the increase in demand for housing and buildings has caused the environmental quality value of ignoring and destroying natural and environmental spaces, especially urban green spaces, and in practice, urban spaces become more areas of financial and economic interactions.

Human beings today, understanding the importance and position of public spaces and areas of recreation and recreation in daily life and the various functions of these spaces among the structure of human gatherings, strive to preserve and revive and make good use of available resources in the planning agenda and Has set its own policies. On the other hand, the lack of attention to socio-cultural approach in the design of such spaces has caused their developmental role to take on an individual aspect and weaken social interactions.

Figure 34. Penang Premium Outlets (Design Village)

Today, the big cities of our country have a long distance with the necessary limits and dimensions in having social spaces, especially in the field of recreational-recreational spaces. Hence, the lack and absence of these spaces will create an unbalanced spirit and an unbalanced pattern of behavior in citizens. Another prominent aspect of the development of recreational and leisure spaces is its economic effects on the exploiting and exploiting society. The effects that are created in the field of job creation and national income through the creation of national and international recreation and tourism areas, have been considered by most managers and decision-makers in the world today and therefore, in recent decades with We have seen significant growth and development of tourism spaces in most countries of the world.

In this regard, the managers and officials of the holy system of the Islamic Republic of Iran, in order to develop the culture of tourism and also to create suitable tourism and recreation areas in the country, have provided appropriate arrangements and contexts and in recent years, support for this sector significantly has increased.

This, in addition to the positive feedback that will bring in the psycho-social spheres, will create the necessary conditions for the development of the tourism industry and subsequently earn national income through the development of the tourism industry, especially in the national and international dimension. The necessity of this arises from the fact that at present, there is a significant shortage in the field of large-scale national and international promenades in the country and the need to develop this sector is undeniable and necessary.

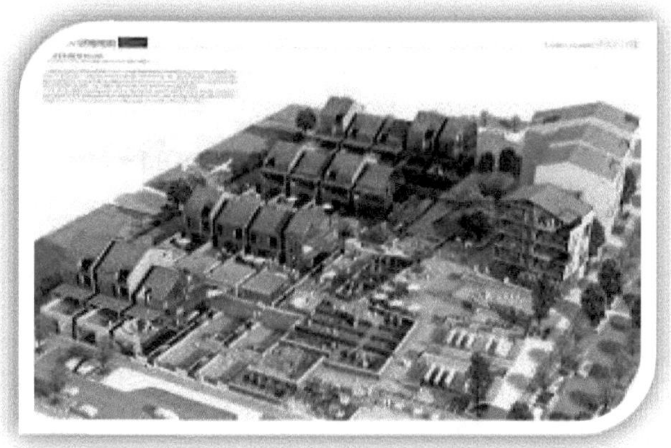

Figure 35. Winner of the Christchurch "Breathe

On the other hand, the creation of recreational and leisure spaces in the inner city, due to the lack of suitable pristine and empty spaces in the inner city, as well as problems such as traffic and pollution caused by the creation of inner-city travel, today is facing many problems. The creation of tourism and recreational spaces in the suburbs of cities and in pleasant climates located in the foothills of nature, is more welcomed.

What we have witnessed in recent years is the great popularity of the residents of the big cities of the country, for suburban trips and turning to recreational-recreational spaces outside the cities. However, recreational-leisure spaces within the city are not so welcomed, because citizens want to leave the city more than anything else. This capability has created a lot of potentials for the development of ecotourism and nature tourism for our country, which, considering the wide popularity of the people, can provide a comprehensive development infrastructure that, if properly managed resources and capital, its positive feedback. It will be shared by the Iranian society.

In this regard, green spaces and recreational-natural recreational spaces outside the city, which are located in the field of human-nature interactions as well as human-human, outside the structural framework of the financial-economic system of large cities, are more important. Among these very important areas in our country, we can mention the green area of Amol city that the site of this project, with its location in the middle of this area, is one of the points with similar potentials. Meanwhile, macro-national policies, based on national planning plans, have placed the northern lands of the country and the provinces of Gilan and Mazandaran to play recreational and ecotourism roles, and therefore, many macro-potentials located in this The region should be directed towards approved macro policies and functions that play recreational-ecotourism and ecotourism roles.

Meanwhile, the strategic position of Mazandaran province and its high potentials in attracting tourists, has caused that this province, despite the low level of investment and lack of tourism development programs in the province, annually receives numerous clients and tourists from different parts of the country and Even other countries. Meanwhile, the site of this project is no exception to this rule and it is obvious that if properly planned and designed, it will certainly strengthen the recreational-ecotourism and ecotourism role defined for the province, taking advantage of the existing advantages. It was able to play a role on a national, regional and international scale.

Figure 36. Room House Plan with Elevation Design | Village House Design | Gopal Architecture | House balcony design, Village house design, 3 room house plan

Establishment of various functions and uses in the project site should be done according to the characteristics of the natural and artificial environment as well as its socio-cultural and economic feedback and the occurrence of social and environmental anomalies in the area should be avoided. This reveals the need for more comprehensive and practical attention to the future development of the project site, and from this perspective, the preparation of development plans with functional, social, environmental and economic considerations will be one of the most important projects of the project so that the complex can have a solid bed. And planned to meet the needs of the region.

Importance of the research topic

The tourism industry has long been with the aim of visiting historical and natural attractions (ecotourism), pilgrimage, trade, use of medical services and . . . It has been formed and gradually developed with the evolution of equipment and the provision of more suitable travel facilities.

Today, this industry is considered as one of the most lucrative activities by all countries. In recent times, due to the development of urbanization and the growth of industry, environmental pollution has increased and has caused the demand for travel and leisure in urban communities to increase. To meet the demand for day-to-day travel, we are witnessing the growth and development of information and communication technologies and services, services, facilities and equipment in the tourism complex in the world.

Because in most countries that have long-term plans to attract tourists, tourist villages have special standards. These studies are necessary for better planning and prevention of many problems in the development of the tourism industry. By studying the tourist villages and also the conditions of their formation, the necessary criteria can be examined and this will lead to the correct design of the tourist village.

In this research, by studying foreign cases and comparing with similar domestic examples, we have achieved the necessary criteria for designing a recreational complex in tourist villages, and by applying it in a practical case study, we will address the necessity of this research.

Figure 37. New urban design for an African village

Research Objectives

The ultimate goal of this project is to design and improve the quality of the tourist village by creating recreational and cultural spaces. Including an efficient fashion system, with appropriate economic returns for society, in order to play a recreational-leisure role, with environmental, functional and socio-cultural considerations, in order to spend leisure time and with the aim of improving the mental, physical and mental dimensions of the population. From it and improving the environmental quality of the project area, in Amol city located in Mazandaran province. From this perspective, the following operational objectives can be proposed in relation to the issue:

Environmental goals

The macro-environmental goal of this project is to provide a physical plan and design system appropriate to the capabilities and environmental capabilities of the project in order to preserve and prevent the destruction of natural lands in the project area and promote its role and environmental position in the limited environmental life. It has a direct impact that can be pursued through the following operational objectives.

- ❖ Reducing the destructive role of development interventions at the land level located within the project area.
- ❖ Creating the necessary bases for the protection and sustainable preservation of natural resources by the people.
- ❖ Creating the necessary conditions for the presence of managed people in national and natural lands in order to prevent the process of destruction of environmental values in the region.
- ❖ Development of green spaces, including afforestation, tree planting, etc., as well as water spaces, including waterways, ponds and reservoirs, in order to soften the air and improve the environmental indicators of the project bed.

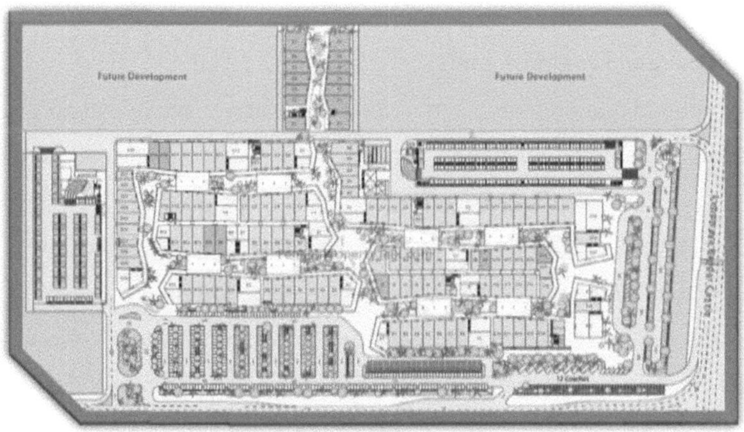

Figure 38. Penang Premium Outlets (Design Village) | Penang Property Talk

Functional goals

The main operational goal of this project is to provide an optimal physical performance plan for the project bed lands, in relation to the capabilities and limitations of the region, in order to create a tourist village to meet the needs and shortcomings in the recreational and ecotourism areas. Which will be achieved through the following operational objectives.

- ❖ Improving the qualitative and quantitative level of site performance in relation to its capabilities and limitations and in relation to and interaction with other spaces and recreational, leisure and sports functions in the province.
- ❖ Analyzing the current functional status of the site and its communications and interactions with neighboring functions and the region index.
- ❖ Creating suitable and worthy landscapes and mirrors on the banks of Haraz River.
- ❖ Establishment of a new center for recreational and leisure activities in Mazandaran province, due to the existing shortcomings.
- ❖ Responding to recreational-leisure needs in the province, by establishing the required functions at an appropriate scale.

Social, cultural and economic goals

The social, cultural and economic purpose of this design is an optimal social, cultural and economic system in accordance with the project area and site of the project, in relation to the demographic structure and social and economic position of the beneficiaries and reducing anomalies and promoting social norms at the domestic level. External is related to the project site as well as the creation of new economic and job opportunities, in a way that ensures positive economic feedback for the project community. This will be pursued through the following operational objectives:

- ❖ Psychological refinement of the users of the project area of influence, by creating a happy and fun atmosphere based on a suitable design.

❖ Creating new job and economic opportunities in order to improve the economic potential of the region's residents by attracting tourists along with creating jobs for the people of the region and designing local markets.

❖ Responding to the recreational-leisure needs of clients in order to regain physical, mental and spiritual strength by designing fun spaces.

❖ Improving the qualities and indicators of control - security and reducing anomalies and social crimes within the site.

❖ Creating the necessary social and cultural backgrounds to prevent the destruction of the environment and pristine and natural space of the project area and the importance of crossing the river through the heart of the city by highlighting the importance and vital role of water in human life by combining water and architecture.

Figure 39. Smart Village Project

To achieve the main goal (design of a tourist village) according to the sub-objectives (physical program, climate studies, study of effective parameters, etc.) steps must be taken. In such a way that it can play a recreational-leisure role with environmental, functional and aesthetic considerations, in order to spend leisure time and with the aim of improving the spiritual, physical and mental dimensions of the population using it and also preserving and protecting pristine spaces natural, pay.

The history of Iranian campuses should be traced back to ancient times. At the same time, the city gardens that were created in Iran during the Safavid period, and especially in Isfahan, were considered as the inspiration of "Ebenezer Howard", the founder of the city garden theory. Obviously, the construction of parks and gardens in the style of European countries in Iran began in the 1970s. (Ebrahimzadeh, 2008: The beginning of attention to urban green space in the West in the meaning and concept of the new industrial era should be sought in the era of the Industrial Revolution and the resulting changes in the political, economic, social and cultural dimensions (Ebrahimzadeh, 3: 2008). Comfort and creating the necessary conditions for a desirable life has always been the goal of human beings. Changes have been made on the planet by human beings in order to create human comfort and well-being. Initially, urban life began with the use of traditional methods to continue living alongside nature, but with the industrialization of urban communities significantly expanded and changed shape. Natural energy mines and forests, now we have to create the conditions for harmony with the environment and creating a sustainable environment. (Rahshahr, 2003: 6)

Definitions of concepts and theories related to the topic

First, we will define the words related to the title, such as entertainment, recreation, recreation, excursion, in order to reach a general acquaintance in this regard, and then we will describe the related titles and their application in the dissertation design section.

Fun

Recreation is any activity or inactivity that is done with the previous intention and with desire in leisure time. Therefore, recreation is an emotional and enjoyable experience that is given to people by their desire in their free time. In other words, when there is not the slightest feeling of compulsion in activity or inactivity in leisure time, this state can definitely be called entertainment. Entertainment is in stark contrast to work in general, and its distinguishing feature is not the aspect of its activity. Rather, it is a state, a state and a feeling in which he touches people and learns them. Every pastime is done in his spare time, but not all of his leisure time is spent just for fun. Activity or inactivity that is without purpose and plan and without previous intention, is not considered part of entertainment. A researcher named Newmin offers this definition ("Recreation refers to any individual or group that takes place in leisure time and because it is a free, voluntary and enjoyable activity, has a special attraction" (Carlsen, Deep and McLean, in his book Recreation in American Life, offers the following definition: 16: 2004).

Figure 40. Holland Village

Recreation

Recreation means the evaluation of leisure time in order to reconstruct and find one's mental and physical self-recreation. Self-reconstruction (reconstruction and reconstruction) of a person mentally and physically is to start a new period of activity-work. (Shafiee Nasab, 2004: 13). Recreation is generally referred to as any kind of entertainment and game activity that is done in this field, whether indoors or outdoors. But all the games and entertainments that are usually done outdoors and outdoors, especially in natural resources, such as walking in nature, watching the scenery of forests and pastures, horseback riding, boating, skiing, camping, picnics. Recreation in open environments requires space and resources. The most suitable resources that can improve the quality of recreation are natural and less modified resources that still retain their aesthetic aspects. Using all forms of parks, regardless of quality, extent or distance and accessibility, means recreation.

Resort

A natural resource for recreation is any natural system, whether water or land, set aside for recreational use. A recreation area can accommodate or use a wide range of natural features from a simple stream to a deep cave. Of the natural systems, the initial condition is to turn it into an actual or potential source of recreation.

Rounds

It is a recreational practical tour that informally uses and motivates consumption, temporal and spatial conditions, economic power, intellectual and cultural level, availability of facilities and personal interests about each individual or group.

Green space and its importance

Aspects of leisure and leisure today, green space has become a valuable national asset that serves the government as a source of capital and directly or indirectly, so that a very close and inseparable relationship between reducing health care costs, increasing health. In general, there is an improvement in quality of life and an increase in average life expectancy with the development of green space and tree planting. (Khademi, 6: 1986). According to the contents expressed in the design, green space also plays an important role, including its importance in the desired career in design, we can name the following items that we must address in the design:

- ❖ The importance of green space in the fight against pollution.
- ❖ The importance of green space in preventing noise pollution.
- ❖ Temperature adjustment.
- ❖ The effect of green space on people's morale.
- ❖ Creative beauty.
- ❖ Permeability and prevention of erosion.

Figure 41. The Urban Village Project: A Vision for Liveable, Sustainable and Affordable Homes

Park

Parks are green spaces designed with different uses for public use, in terms of research, education, recreation and maintaining the health of the environment and people. In fact, parts and tissues of the city that the public has physical and visual access to and activities in takes place. In fact, it is a place to spend leisure time, interaction, conversation, education and so on. (Country Management and Planning Organization, 2001: 26)

 In his Ecological Glossary, Richard Carpenter defines the word "parkland" as "an area in which trees are scattered in groups or individually in a bed of grass cover." More than any other term, it refers to natural lands with scattered trees and quasi-forests that have the potential for a specific type of recreational activity.

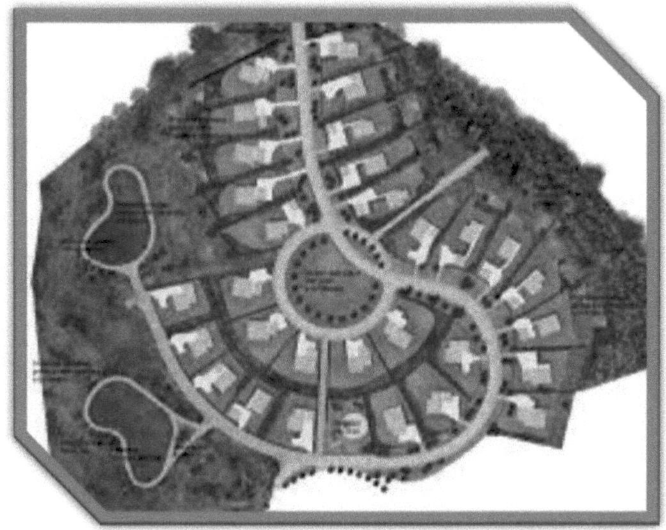

Figure 42. Kypeside Eco Village - TGP Landscape Architects

The following definitions in different cultures show a corner of the characteristics of the park. Parks are usually spaces that have a variety of uses at the same time limited and indeterminate and with a flexible form and minimal construction and maximum use of natural materials for walking. Rest, entertainment, thinking, playing, etc. are established. (Izadpanah Jahromi, 2002: 11) According to the definition of the park, the existence of such an atmosphere is necessary in the design of the village, and parks with special titles such as children's park, women's park can be designed in different parts of it.

Water and architecture

Throughout history, our architects have incorporated water into their collections and used a treasure trove of physical, religious, and mythological features to enrich their architecture. Before the advent of Islam in Iran, architecture was present along the water and in the midst of nature without disturbing it. The role of water was more of an abstract role, shrines (Anahita temples, fire temples, etc.) were formed next to water and finally respect for the existence of water.

It was as if water and fire coexisted peacefully and celebrated their grandeur. Examples of this can be seen in Azargashnast Fire Temple and Karian fire temple. Water plays a major role in the formation of the Iranian garden and trees, plants and flowers have the most important role after water, the presence of which has its roots in water. The presence of water in the Iranian garden shapes the character of the surrounding environment. The parks are gone. Parallel and vertical networking with the river axis spreads throughout the city and streets and blocks form a building. In fact, bridges act as intermediaries. In Isfahan, the Armenian region of Jolfa is located on the other side of the Zayandeh River and connects thirty-three bridges in this region to other parts of the city.

The site to be designed in Amol city is located in a place that is adjacent to the bridge in two directions and the river in one direction. Bridges often have a prominent urban location and if they are attractive, they will become a symbol of the city, such as Khajoo Bridge and 33 bridges and suspension bridges in Amol. Unlike fountains, springs and rivers, which are inherently kinetic elements, reservoirs and ponds are calm elements that collect water from the water cycle.

Five bridges cross the Haraz River inside the city of Amol, all of which are bridges connecting the two main parts of the city.

As mentioned, they have a prominent urban location, especially the suspension bridge next to the site for design, which can be used in the design of the arch design style, such as bridge piers. And because of the historical values of bridges, it is better for the designed buildings to be in harmony with them in terms of height and appearance.

Stagnant water naturally reflects images and, due to its reflectivity, is a determining factor in composition. Their mirror surface accepts the surroundings and then reflects. In our architecture, pools are used as a symbol of stagnant water and with their regular geometric shapes, they balance the building. The pools in front of the building complement the architecture and reflect them like a mirror, a clear example of which is Isfahan Chehelston.

Figure 43. Massimo Iosa Ghini's colorful Muscovite neighborhood in Russia

Another suggestion that can be expressed for the design of the area is the use of the same ponds and fountains, which by combining the river and entering the site into the site, we combine it with architecture. Contrast is beauty.

Theories

Tourism (tourism and its types)

Tourism, as defined by the World Tourism Organization (WTO), refers to activities that go to places outside of their normal environment for leisure, work, and other purposes. Tourism in its broadest definition includes people who travel in connection with their work and profession and those who carry out scientific and research activities. In this way, the scope of tourism's impact on the environment and its impact on the environment becomes much wider. Tourism is also a set of interactions that occur in the process of attracting and hosting, between tourists, travel agencies, governments of origin, host governments and local people.

Figure 44. Urban design of A-Qahad heritage village

Tourism is a multidimensional category and is related to several factors. Major and influential factors in the tourism industry are: tourists, countries of origin, destination governments, indigenous peoples, tourism organizations (domestic and international travel agencies), educational institutions (universities and technical and professional organizations), service organizations (hotels, hotels), hotels, hotels Economic infrastructure (roads, sewerage network, communication networks), transportation network (air, land), tourist attractions (historical, natural, cultural ...) all these factors under the influence of environmental factors such as cultural and social factors, Political and security, economic, technology and environmental. (Zahedi, 4: 2006)

Typology of tourism (tourism)

In this section, several types of tourism classification are mentioned so that after getting acquainted with its different types, it is possible to determine the type of tourism desired in this design and design it based on their needs:

Mass tourism

Mass tourism is a common commercial tourism that exists on a large scale around the world. Such tourism activities are carried out by large tourism companies and have their own markets, which are usually concentrated in certain areas of the world. Mass tourism varies in terms of travel motivation and destination of choice. In this type of tourism, tourists are looking for originality, novelty and diversity in the neighborhoods visited.

Fam tourism or cultural tourism, ecotourism and adventure

The word fam consists of the initials of the words cultural, ecotourism and adventure. In this classification, tourism is divided into three categories. In cultural tourism, the tourist's goal is to visit the ceremonies, characteristics, and cultural manifestations of the host community.

Figure 45. The Urban Village Project

Normal tourism and nature tourism

In this classification, tourism is divided into two categories: normal tourism and naturalistic tourism. Although all types of tourism are somehow related to nature, but in this classification, the end use is not intended. Historical tourism and pilgrimage tourism overlap.

Normal tourism

Ordinary tourism is a type of tourism whose chosen destination does not necessarily have to do with nature. This type of tourism can in turn be divided into several sub-types.

Historical and ancient tourism

In this type of tourism, tourists pay attention to historical attractions and antiquities, such as: Persepolis in Iran, the Three Pyramids in Egypt, historical monuments in Rome and Greece.

Pilgrimage tourism

In this type of tourism, places of pilgrimage and religious ceremonies and rituals are considered by tourists, such as pilgrimage to the Kaaba, Jerusalem and Mashhad. Examples of religious ceremonies and rituals that attract the attention of some tourists are: Ashura mourning and carpet weaving.

Cultural tourism

Many tourists are interested in visiting and attending cultural and artistic ceremonies and adjust their itinerary to match the season of these rituals and ceremonies. Participation in art programs such as music, opera and theater concerts can also be included in this category.

Sports tourism

Some tourists, in order to get rid of the monotonous life throughout their work and occupation, are looking for a time and place to be required to do sports, while others decide to travel to visit visas and sports competitions and visit places that have special sports facilities. Sports tourism has a long history The World Olympic Games are a clear example of sports tourism, which attracts a large number of tourists and provides a rich income for the host countries.

Meet relatives and friends

The purpose of some trips is to visit friends and acquaintances. Of course, in addition to these visits, there may also be visits to tourist attractions, but the main focus of these trips is to meet relatives and acquaintances.

Medical tourism

Natural tourism includes those tourism activities that deal directly with natural resources and attractions.

Natural tourism can be classified into six sub-categories:

- ❖ Coastal tourism
- ❖ Adventure tourism
- ❖ Consumer tourism
- ❖ Closed Tourism
- ❖ Health Tourism
- ❖ Ecotourism

Here is a brief description of each of these types:

Coastal or sand tourism

This type of tourism is closely related to the recreation of the Mediterranean coast, parts of the Pacific Ocean and Southeast Asia. In fact, this type of tourism with its uncontrolled development has caused negative economic, cultural, social and environmental effects in these areas. In Iran, the indiscriminate and reckless use of natural resources of the country's coasts and the imposition of contaminated waste and waste to these areas has caused irreparable damage to the environment of the region.

Figure 46. Arpadaresi Tourist Village Project | Alireza Mashhadi Mirza Architects

Adventurous tourism

Adventure tourism is a type of tourism that is somewhat risky and requires physical activity and special skills. Examples of this tourism are: water skiing, mountaineering, sailing, caving, which in all of these activities, nature, it is challenging and these efforts are accompanied by excitement.

Consumer tourism

In all types of tourism, there is a general consumption factor. But consumer tourism refers to activities that lead to the consumption and damage of natural resources. The most common types of consumer tourism are fishing and hunting. This type of tourism has faced many criticisms. Among other things, killing animals from an environmental point of view disrupts the biological balance.

Enclosed tourism

Enclosed tourism refers to the type of tourism that keeps elements of the natural environment under special and controlled conditions and exposes them to tourists, such as zoos, aquariums, and bird cages.

Health Tourism

Health tourism is a type of tourism that is related to health and medical activities and is considered by tourists who pay attention to the healing properties of natural resources such as: hot springs of medicinal plants, sludge beaches and medicinal grasses.

Ecotourism

There are several definitions of ecotourism, some of which are mentioned here:

- Visit an area to see the land, animals and plants intact in that area.
- Travel to nature in a way that while protecting the ecosystem, the dignity of local communities is also respected. In this definition, in addition to natural resources, the values of local people have been considered and the need to create a balance between natural resources, tourism, local community and tourists has been considered.
- Hector Ceballos-Lascurian Hector Ceballos-Lascurian was one of the first to define ecotourism in the 1980s. "Cultural manifestations of the past and present of indigenous peoples."
- The Environmental Advisory Council of Canada recognizes ecotourism as a nature travel experience that helps protect the ecosystem while preserving the host community.
- The definition provided by the Australian National Ecotourism Institute is: "Natural tourism, which combines education and environmental awareness and is managed in an environmentally sound manner."
- The International Union for Conservation of Nature (IUCN) defines ecotourism as follows:

❖ "Ecotourism is the responsible travel to relatively pristine natural areas in order to enjoy nature in a way that has few negative effects on nature and provides the basis for socio-economic participation of the indigenous population."

❖ The International Ecotourism Society (IES) definition of ecotourism is:

❖ "Ecotourism is responsible travel to natural areas that protects the environment and ensures the well-being of local people." (Zahedi, 2006: 4-17)

❖ According to the explanations given, the type of tourism that should be considered for the design of the desired village is naturalistic tourism of the ecotourism type and part of the coast, considering that environmental protection is one of our design approaches.

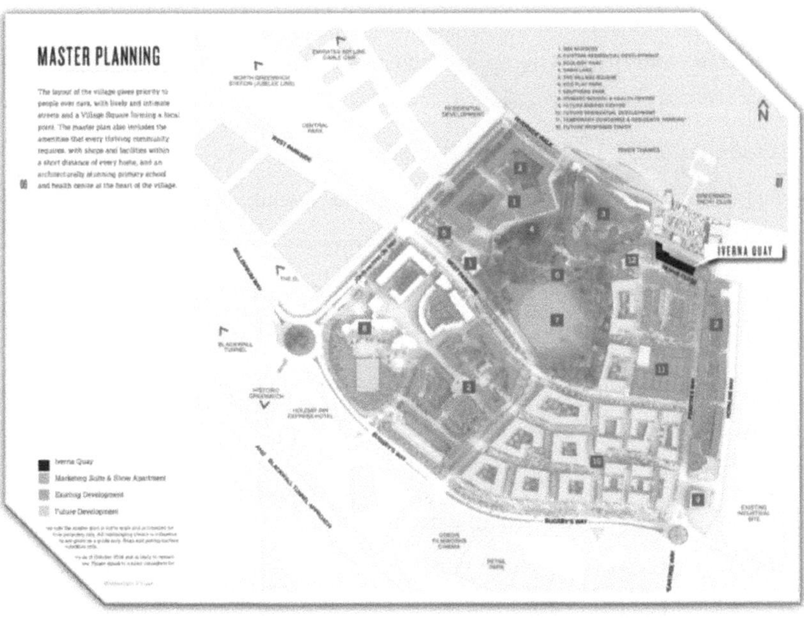

Figure 47. Designing for community: An analysis of Greenwich Millennium Village

Generalities and definitions of tourist village

In order to study the design of a tourist village, we must first examine the generalities and concepts of tourist villages, their types and functions, and the conditions for their creation. In this part of this study, we will examine the concepts of tourist villages with reference to foreign examples.

Definition of tourist village

There are places in a province that place or distances close to it in terms of natural, cultural and historical attractions have the necessary capabilities to attract tourists and need to establish facilities and facilities for tourism and information. The tourist village, as a center for the concentration of domestic tourists in order to make leisure, holiday and residential trips within the province to various tourist attractions throughout the province, can be a center for accommodation and distribution of tourists in each province. Therefore, this center should have all the features needed by residents, tourists and those who spend their leisure time in the village. Therefore, the construction of recreational, sports, service and welfare spaces to the level of world standards today is envisaged to create a village.

Observance of environmental considerations and sustainable development are other characteristics that should be considered in the proposed plans. In this case, we can be sure that the construction of such villages will have a good return, both economically and culturally. The goals that the tourist village is supposed to be known for are:

- ❖ Increasing the number of tourists in an area.
- ❖ Increasing public revenue from tourism development.
- ❖ Increasing job opportunities.
- ❖ Realizing the potential tourism capacities in a region.
- ❖ Attracting more private sector participation in tourism development.
- ❖ Increasing investment attraction.
- ❖ Improving the level of public services to tourists (Tourism Zones Organization, 2002).

Tourist villages are areas that have some characteristics of a place as a subject of tourism. In this area, the customs and culture of the local communities are still intact and pristine. The tourist village is also a combination of some protection and conservation factors in which, in addition to preserving nature and the environment, items such as cooking methods, traditional agricultural systems and local communities are preserved.

Creating and providing suitable facilities for turning a place as a tourist destination is of special importance. They are places to enjoy their vacation in this place. These places have spaces or spaces have been created in them that make visitors experience interesting and memorable moments in a space different from where they live. In the following, we will introduce the types of tourist villages to determine the desired type in the design.

Types of tourist village

Tourist villages are classified into different types according to the natural capabilities where they are located and built, as well as according to different maps and functions. Depending on the amount of facilities and attractions around, tourist villages may have accommodation or include only limited uses.

Figure 3. The Layout of the Village Close-up. the Layout of the River of the Old Town and Houses Editorial Photography - Image of european, mini: 140506227

After reviewing, we come to the conclusion that the village in question is of a design type.

Healthy towns and villages

Health tourism is a type of travel that, in addition to entertainment, leisure and comfort, also brings health and medical care. Currently, medical tourism is one of the fastest growing sectors of the tourism industry in the world and is rapidly becoming a global industry. In the whole world, out of the total number of people who enter countries as tourists (international tourists), seven percent are those who have taken action to treat and use the natural gifts of that country.

Areas of activity in the field of health tourism in the world include: Mineral spas (Health Spa), Weight management programs (Program Weight Management), Cosmetic and Plastic Surgery (Cosmetic and Plastic Surgery), Knee replacement surgery, ... (Knee replacement), Coronary By-Pass Surgery, Organ Transplant, Lasik Surgery, Dental Implantation, Rehabilitation and Recuperation, etc. Leading regions in the field of health tourism in the world can be Bahrain, Singapore, Cuba, Costa Rica, Hungary, Jordan, Lithuania, Malaysia, Thailand, Belgium, Poland, Turkey, Dubai, USA, South Africa and India. cited. (Zahedi, 17: 2006)

Coastal Village

Coastal villages are usually referred to as suburban areas that are formed and located in coastal areas that have the ability to attract tourists. Like the coastal village of Panormo in Greece, which was originally a small village but many factors have made it a tourist village. In coastal villages, the main factor of formation is proximity or proximity to the beach (Shahraki, 2011: 29) that the village in design is close to this type of village in terms of some features.

Mountain village

Mountain villages that are formed in mountainous areas usually have the ability to create mountain resorts, and depending on the geographical and climatic conditions, there can be activities such as skiing, snowboarding, mountaineering, rock climbing, rock climbing, snow climbing, snow climbing and hiking (Shahraki, 31: 2011).

Figure 48. Eco Village, Design Educates Awards

Desert villages

Desert villages are formed in desert areas. These villages have residences for activities such as stargazing, sand safaris using special equipment, camel riding, ostrich riding, familiarity with herbal and wildlife medicines. Countries that have worked to locate and equip desert areas to develop the tourism industry include the UAE and the deserts around Dubai (Shahraki, 33: 2011). According to the mentioned cases, the type of village intended for design is almost of the type of coastal villages.

Tourism

The position and function of tourism in urban life

Probably the most places where tourism takes place are cities. Urbanization, which is the most complex human achievement today, has different physical, social, economic, cultural and anthropological dimensions. The circle will be more affected by the mentioned factors. Leisure, recreation and tourism are words that everyone has heard or used many times. Leisure is equivalent to leisure for most of us, but recreation is the activities that are done to spend leisure time. The word tourism is often in the mind. We associate travel, vacation and scenic scenery.

Traveling to cities and using public spaces for entertainment and leisure attracts tourists to parks, cinemas, museums, shopping malls, various gardens and exhibitions, shrines and buildings and sights. There is a difference between spending leisure time for citizens and tourists and CIA tourists because spending leisure time for tourists requires travel, so the type of demand is also different. (Imran Zaveh, 2003: 90)

The structure of a city that focuses on tourism is different from an ordinary city. Establishment of accommodation and hotels, leisure centers, library facilities, catering and guidance in urban sightseeing centers and transportation should all be formed in accordance with tourism relations. The more appropriate the arrangement of these factors, the easier the cultural exchange caused by CIA Hatgari is located in the area of the site for the design of the city hotel, which in terms of capacity to respond to clients and the need, the accommodation in this village responds. It is also responsive in terms of the need for cultural spaces despite the cinema with two halls and a museum in the very close margin of this site, but it is suggested to use the axes that come from them to design the site to somehow coordinate this function in the site. The plan showed.

Figure 49. OPEN Architecture Designs a Village for Learning in Shanghai

Ecotourism

As we know, man and nature are inseparable combinations. Man is born in nature, lives in nature and dies in nature. All natural features including natural forests, national wildlife parks, rivers and nature around them especially waterfalls, mountains, natural springs, summers, hunting areas, fishing in, seas and lakes and surrounding habitats, habitats Indigenous as well as natural caves determine the extent of nature tourism.

The International Ecotourism Society defines ecotourism as: "A responsible trip to natural areas that, while protecting the environment, brings health to local communities as well." Ecotourism is actually a journey to a natural area, a journey that is beneficial to local communities. A journey that has led man to a deep understanding of nature and the environment and to protect the protection of biodiversity. (Kiarostami, 2003: 33).

Ecotourism is composed of a combination of the word's ecology and tourism and in fact is the product of many challenges between extremists advocate the use and unlimited use of nature and supporters of rational use of these resources, which in Persian means medicine tourism is environmental. (Amirani, 2003: 4) Ecotourism is a new phenomenon that shows only a part of the entire tourism industry and is based on purposeful travel to relatively natural areas to study, enjoy, spiritual use of landscapes and any kind of contemporary or past cultural activity in these areas that our main goal in this design dissertation according to the ecological approach is also in line with these criteria, so we will give a brief explanation in this regard.

The term became popular in 1965 and introduced four criteria for ecotourism.

- ❖ Minimal negative impact on the environment.
- ❖ Minimal negative impact on culture and maximum responsibility towards the culture of the host community.
- ❖ Maximum economic benefit for the host community.
- ❖ Maximum recreational satisfaction for the participation of tourists.

Today, on a global scale, it is accepted that ecotourism should be related to environmental protection and appropriate and long-term use of nature, with minimal changes in the balance of the natural environment and harm (Mohammadi, 2003: 17)

Sustainable ecotourism

The basis of ecotourism is how tourists can visit natural and cultural resources to promote, raise awareness and spend their leisure time and enjoyment without having a negative impact on these resources. Conservation of recreational resources, along with productivity, is very sensitive. Sustainable management of recreational resources is synonymous with the term sustainable ecotourism.

Ecotourism is a type of tourist management in which the ecological system is protected. Protection and improvement of the natural environment and preparation of executive plans to promote natural beauty by developing green space and creating recreational areas in nature, such as picnic areas, camping, rest combined with multifunctional information systems to enhance the knowledge of users. Environmental protection will be one of the goals of the ecotourism development plan. The great recreational potential of forest and national parks, etc., and their special place in the tourism industry in the development of ecotourism are considered.

The main claim of ecotourism proponents is that ecotourism is based on stimulus strategies, practical strategies and preventive measures by activating and exploiting the sensitive natural areas themselves and promotes sustainable development. Because by doing so, it keeps such areas out of the scope of employment and the threat of aggressive development operations of the human environment. And the threat of aggressive human development operations to be protected. Therefore, and according to the ecological design approach, one of the proposed solutions is to design buildings with a small volume of minimal and low interference in the site.

The concept of sustainable tourism is an acceptable and praiseworthy method that, while meeting the recreational needs of current tourists, must also take into account the fact that the affected areas also belong to future generations and must be used properly. Preserve them in such a way that our children can also touch these precious gems. Proper use of ecotourism or environmental tourism can have a positive effect on environmental protection in addition to socio-economic benefits, for example, proper land use keeps the land covered. Remain from its native plants and in addition to numerous internal economic benefits, attract many tourists and lead to domestic and foreign investment in the country's infrastructure and ultimately sustainable development. (Mohammadi, 19: 2003)

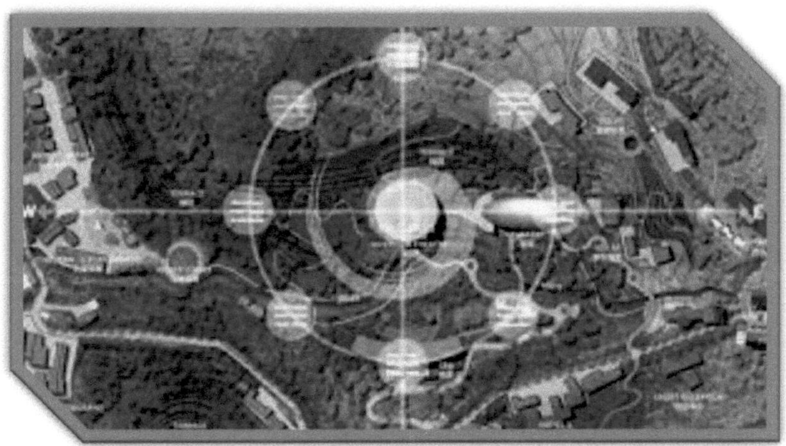

Figure 50. SASSEUR Eco-tourist Village, « Inhabitant, Green Design, Innovation, Architecture, Green Building

Iran and tourist villages

In order to build tourist villages in environmental areas; Based on the agreement between the Cultural Heritage and Tourism Organization and the Environmental Protection Organization in 2001, a three-axis network of tourist villages has been identified. The base of this network was formed in three axes of Alborz, Zagros and Kavir with special features of these areas and tourists who want this climate. The Lut Desert passes through northwestern-southeastern Qatar, a route to Europe to Pakistan and India, which is thought to be the best route for European tourists and creates special attractions for this group.

The Zagros axis is a route in the north-southern heights of Iran that passes through the provinces of Kurdistan, Kermanshah, Lorestan, Chaharmahal, Fars and Bushehr and includes the characteristics and attractions of nomadic and indigenous life; A route that has special attractions even for domestic tourists. Alborz axis is a route in the east-west of Iran, which passes through the provinces of Azerbaijan, Gilan, Mazandaran, Golestan and Khorasan and currently has the largest share in domestic tourism in Iran and annually hosts more than 20 million people is a domestic tourist.

The desert axis includes the tourist villages of Qom Wandering Island, Taft Yazd and Mahan Kerman, and the Zagros axis includes the tourist villages of Shurab Lorestan, Koohrang Chaharmahal, Biston Kermanshah, Maharloo Fars and Shif Island of Bushehr. Alborz axis has the tourist villages of Ashuradeh Island, Gaz Port and Turkmen Port in Golestan, Gisum Forest Park in Gilan, Islamic Island in East Azerbaijan and Neishabour in Khorasan to join the promise of tourist villages. (Rahshahr International Group, 2009: 75)

Check the status quo

What we are witnessing in recent years is the great attention of the residents of the big cities of the country to suburban travel and turning to recreational spaces outside the cities, while the recreational spaces within the city are not so welcomed, because the citizens more than everything intends to leave the city by creating attractiveness in inner city areas by expanding and activating inner city spaces, this attention can be created.

Figure 51. Crazy Conceptual Design for Biomimetic Eco-Village in Belgium

The strategic position of Mazandaran province and its high potentials in attracting tourists, has caused that this province, despite the low level of investment and lack of tourism development programs in the province, annually receives many clients and tourists from different parts of the country and even other countries. Meanwhile, the site in question of this project is no exception to this rule and it is obvious that if properly planned and designed, certainly in order to strengthen the recreational and ecotourism role defined for the province, taking advantage of the existing advantages, will be able to play a role on a national, regional scale.

Establishment of various functions and uses in the project site should be done according to the characteristics of the natural and artificial environment as well as its socio-cultural and economic feedback and the occurrence of social and environmental anomalies in the area should be avoided.

Figure 52. Design Village Outlet Mall - NS Bluescope Malaysia

The ultimate goal of this dissertation is to design parts of a village with a homogeneous, balanced and efficient function in Amol city with appropriate economic effects for the residents of the region, in the form of a function interacting with human society, so that it can play a recreational role. Leisure and ecotourism with environmental, functional and aesthetic considerations, in order to spend leisure time and with the aim of promoting the spiritual, physical and mental dimensions of the population using it and also preserving pristine and natural spaces. What seems to be important in this process is to pay attention to the ecological approach of the complex, in its environmental, physical dimensions.

Necessities and advantages of the project

❖ The need to lay the groundwork and create a recreational area in the city to attract native and non-native tourists to the city.

❖ Predicting the widespread acceptance of the project by tourists.

❖ The need for environmental development of the project area in order to protect water and soil resources and plant and animal life and ecological values of the area and improve the quality of life and living in neighboring areas and under direct influence (as environmental affected areas).

❖ Existence of urban security margin for citizens and residents.

The need for preservation and protection of natural resources

Among the strategic goals of development interventions in the lands of the project area is the need to protect and preserve the environmental resources located in the lands of the project area and the need to prevent the process of existing destruction.

Figure 53. SASSEUR Eco-tourist Village by HEIMdesign « Inhabitat – Green Design, Innovation, Architecture, Green Building

References

Armaghan, Simin. 2007. The book Tourism and its Role in Geography, Islamic Azad University, Islamshahr Branch, Faculty Member, Islamic Azad University, Islamshahr Branch.

Meteorological Department of Semnan Province, 2007. Climatic Zoning of the Province, Volume 3.

Eftekhari and Mahdavi, 2006, Intervention in old and dilapidated urban contexts (history and backgrounds) Special Letter No. 14 of the Municipalities of the Ministry of Interior, Municipalities Organization.

Bakhtiari, Saeed. 2002, Atlas of Iranian Roads (Institute of Geography and Cartography of Geology).

Papli Yazdi, Mohammad Hussein. Saghaei, Mehdi 2006. Tourism (nature and concepts). Publications of the Ministry of Culture and Islamic Guidance.

Taqvaee, Massoud, Ahmadi, Abdul Hussein. 2003, Determining and analyzing the levels of enjoyment of cities, villages and districts of Kermanshah province, Quarterly Journal of Rural and Development, Publications of the Research Center for Rural Issues. The sixth year. Nos. 1 and 2.

Tavassoli, Mahmoud, 2008, Quarterly Journal of Urban Development and Improvement, Haft Shahr, Ministry of Housing and Urban Development No. 2.

Jedari Eyvazi, Jamshid. 2004. Geomophology of Iran, Payame Noor University Press.

Javan, Jafar. Summer 2000. Quarterly Journal of Population and Development. Publications of the Civil Registration Organization. No. 32

Jahandoost, Rasoul (Master of Geography, University of Tehran), Koohstani, Ghasem (Master of Civil Engineering, Khajeh Nasir al-Din Tusi University), 2008, city tourism and its effects on television and urban space, geography site.

Hafiz Nia, Mohammad Reza. 2004. Introduction to research method in humanities, Samat Publications.

Habibi, Seyed Mohsen. 2008. The book from the city to the city (a historical analysis of the concept of the city and its physical appearance and thinking and impact), University of Tehran Press.

Romina, Nadia. 2005. Master Thesis; A Study of Land Use Developments in the Old Texture (Case Study of Semnan), Supervisor; Yousef Ali Ziari, Consultant; Zeinab Karkabadi.

Hamshahri newspaper, Wednesday, October 20, 2010, tourist definition, website www.hamshahrionline.com

Iran Independent Morning Newspaper, July 4, 2007, Afarinesh Sanandaj, Afarinesh Reporter.

Rawal, Raj, Winter 2000. Architecture rises from the heart of society and people, Abadi Magazine. Seventh year. Nos. 27 and 28, special building festival.

Goli, Ali, Saghaei, Mehdi, Ezatollah Humafi, September 7, 2009, Application of MS_SWOT model in tourism management, Case study of Mashhad metropolis, Journal of Geography and Development, No. 14.

Ebrahimzadeh, A., Ebadi Jokandan, 2008, An analysis of the spatial distribution of green space use in the three urban areas of Zahedan, 39, Journal of Geography and Development, No. 11.

Amirani, Mohammad Hadi, 2003, Green Journey and Reflection on the Concepts and Benefits of Ecotourism, Jihad Monthly, Deputy for Extension and Exploitation System, No. 261, page 4.

Khademi, Mostafa, 1986, Green Space, Ministry of Program and Budget (Industrial Management), pp. 5-6.

Zahedi, Shams al-Sadat, 2006, Fundamentals of Tourism and Sustainable Vacotourism (with Emphasis on Environment) First Edition, Allameh Tabatabaei University Press, page 4.

Zandpour, Mehdi, 2003, Histo-Ecological Tourism Center, Master Thesis, Tehran University of Science and Technology.

Management and Planning Organization of the country, 2001, Green space design criteria, (Office of Education and Development of Criteria) First Edition.

Cultural Heritage Organization of Handicrafts and Tourism, 2002, National Committee of Nature Tourism of Iran Compilation of national document on development and management of nature tourism in the country.

Handicrafts and Tourism Cultural Heritage Organization of Mazandaran Province, 2008.

Shaygan, Dariush, 2001, New Enchantment, translated by Fatemeh Valiani, second edition, Farzan Rooz Publishing.

Shahandeh, Behzad, 2001, Ecotourism is not only nature tourism, Green Wave Volume, No. 7.

Gilan Shahran Civil Company, 2008, Comprehensive plan of Shahran national tourism sample area, first volume.

Shariatnejad, Shamsollah, Sharifi, Morteza, 2009, Preliminary planning for ecotourism development, Quarterly Journal of Forests and Rangelands, Forests and Rangelands Organization, No. 34.

Kiarostami, Ghasem, The Necessity of Ecotourism Development to Prevent the Destruction of Valleys and Paradise Northeast of Tehran, Page 33, Payame Sabz Monthly, Third Year, No. 23.

Memarian, Gholamhossein, 2005, Introduction to Iranian residential architecture Extroverted typology, Tehran, University of Science and Technology Press.

Mansouri, Ali, 2002, Tourism and Sustainable Development, Journal of Geography Education Growth, No. 63.

Printed by Books on Demand GmbH, Norderstedt / Germany